D1553583

LEADVILLE

By Christian J. Buys

**WESTERN REFLECTIONS
PUBLISHING COMPANY**®

Lake City, Colorado

To

Sherlock, Treff, Tai, Siska, Jackson, Cholla, Arrow, and Elvis

For all the joy and companionship

ISBN 978-1-932738-00-1

Library of Congress Control Number: 2003115768

Cover illustration: *Frank Leslie's Illustrated Newspaper,* June 7, 1879.
(A "swell" arrives in Leadville.)
Cover and text design by Laurie Goralka Design

Second Edition
Printed in the United States of America

Western Reflections Publishing Company®
P. O. Box 1149
951 N. Highway 149
Lake City, CO 81235
www.westernreflectionspub.com

Table Of Contents

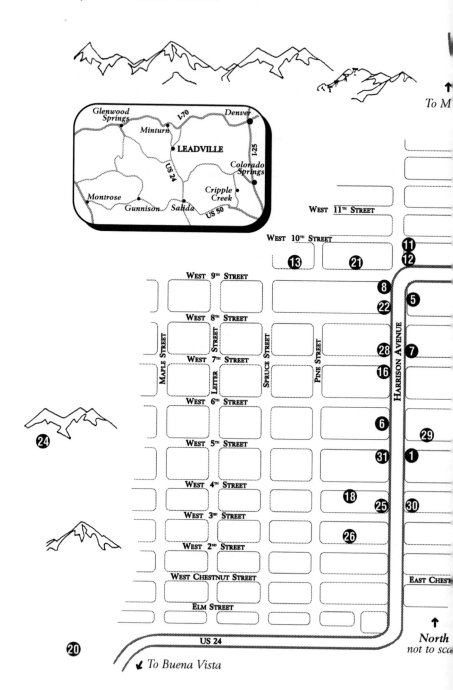

MAP **v**

LEADVILLE

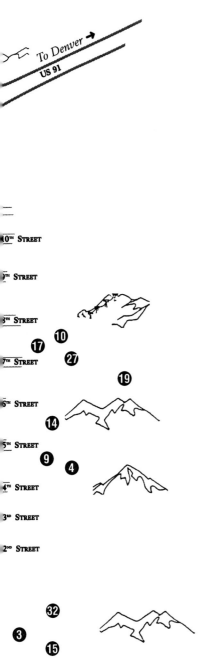

1. American National Bank
2. Annunciation Church
3. California Gulch
4. Carbonate Hill
5. City Hall
6. Courthouse
7. Delaware Hotel
8. Englebach House
9. Finntown
10. Fryer Hill
11. Healy House
12. Heritage Museum
13. King House
14. Little Jony Mine
15. Long and Derry Hill
16. Masonic Temple
17. Matchless Mine
18. Millionaires Row
19. Mosquito Mountains
20. National Fish Hatchery
21. National Mining Hall of Fame
22. Presbyterian Church
23. Saint Vincent's Hospital (old)
24. Sawatch Mountains
25. Silver Dollar Saloon
26. State Street (2nd St.)
27. Stumpftown
28. Tabor Grand Hotel
29. Tabor House
30. Tabor Opera House
31. Western Hardware
32. Yak Tunnel

Acknowledgements

My deepest appreciation goes to Nancy Manly who meticulously reviewe my manuscript, suggested several excellent content changes, corrected m historical errors (any that remain are entirely mine), and guided me to sev eral images in the Colorado Mountain History Collection in the Lak County Public Library. Barb Bost graciously allowed me access to an arra of wonderful archival material as well as reviewed the last two chapter Bruce McCalister, a connoisseur of Leadville history, patiently spent tim with me searching his, and his wife Hillery's, extensive collection of pho tographs. I am also indebted to Rita Eisenheim for adroitly editing the firs draft of this manuscript. Thanks also to Laurie Goralka Casselberry for he exemplary art direction, design, and production. As for my close friend and publishers, P. David and Jan Smith, without their incredibly generou help and support, this book would not have seen the light of day.

CHAPTER ONE

Early Years (1860s-1870s)

L eadville towers, literally and figuratively, over most mining boom towns in America. Nestled in the two-mile-high Arkansas Valley, which lies between awe-inspiring mountain ranges, the Cloud City's environs surpass all the superlatives that have been used to describe it. Each clear morning as the rising sun inches over the magnificent heights of the Mosquito Mountain Range to the east, its first rays illuminate the even more impressive peaks of the Sawatch Range to the west. As this timeless source of light continues slowly to traverse the sky, it peels back the dark from the lush Arkansas Valley that connects these two spectacular geological bookends. Once the sun fully clears the Mosquito Range, the warmth of its rays is welcomed by Leadville which hugs the eastern side of the valley. Making its way along an invisible arc, the sun — now a perfect blazing circle — becomes an active artist, subtly changing the hues and definitions of this indescribably beautiful setting. In the early evening, as it plunges behind the crenelated peaks of the Sawatch Range, Leadville shivers briefly, bracing itself for another crisp, cold night.

There was a time, however, when Leadville neither stopped to admire its surroundings nor shivered as the sun set, even in the depth of winter. Those were the boom days. Frenetic, bawdy times in the late 1870s when thousands upon thousands of miners and entrepreneurs of almost every description and ethical inclination transformed this portion of the pristine valley into what looked like a giant gopher colony. Massive mounds of bright-colored earth were churned up and spit out helter-skelter. Magnificent stands of trees became seas of stumps. Hundreds of tents, cabins, and ramshackle buildings seemingly sprang up overnight and everywhere. Masses of fortune seekers jammed the muddy streets and paths twenty-four hours a day. Everyone in America — or so it seemed — wanted a piece of the action. After all, this was Leadville. This was the boom town of boom towns.

For a few years the silver-ore discoveries lived up to the exhilaration and fantasies of those early Leadvillites. Real fortunes were unearthed as enduring legends were created. But it did not last long, and frankly, very few struck it rich. Indeed, given the perspective which comes with time, many now view Leadville's legacy as yet another land grab from the Native Americans. They also point out that this frenzied attack on the earth ultimately bequeathed us a nightmare of environmental pollution. So goes American hindsight. Nevertheless, the colorful and checkered legacy of Leadville has few rivals in America for sheer excitement and energy. And it all started with one man searching for a dream in the middle of nowhere.

Traditional historical wisdom holds that it was Abe Lee who in April 1860 first dipped his pan into the nearly frozen creek about 100 miles west of Denver City, Kansas Territory. A few clusters of hardy and hopeful prospectors, including Lee, had spread out across the valley floor in search of gold. They agreed that if anyone made a "strike," they would signal the others by firing four shots and building a large fire.

Here we should remind ourselves that when Abe Lee joined "the company of Georgians in the summer of 1859 [1860?]" (*The* [Denver] *Daily News*, January 19, 1902) that struck out toward present-day Arkansas Valley, there was nothing in the way of "civilization" in this region.

Prospectors were basically on their own — with few sources of food or shelter. All their camping supplies, prospecting equipment, and most of their food had to be carried in or packed on mules. Their very lives depended on primitive, heavy equipment, and clothing that any modern mountain backpacker would consider wholly inadequate and downright dangerous. One unfortunate slip by mule or man also meant trouble, big trouble. If a prospector didn't plummet to his death off some narrow rock-strewn trail, a sprained ankle, or worse yet a major broken bone, meant certain agony and possibly death. They simply could not afford to become ill. Further, many prospectors came from east of the Mississippi and nothing in the East could have prepared them for the sheer scale of the West. Their first look at the Rockies must have taken them aback. For there before their unbelieving eyes loomed the most powerful and forbidding geological phenomenon they had ever seen. Once they crossed into one of the gulches in present-day Arkansas Valley they might as well have been on another planet. It was that remote and threatening to anyone but the most adventuresome.

In spite of these daunting obstacles, between 1860 and 1880 thousands of fortune seekers spread out across present-day Colorado. Viewed from above, this throng must have looked like an army of starving ants slowly surging into nearly impenetrable terrain. What happened at Leadville, although not on such a grand scale, occurred all over the Rocky Mountains. At first, small groups of prospectors like the Georgians groped their way along the unexplored contours of the Rocky Mountains. If they struck precious metal, like Lee did, they stayed where they found it. A trickle of prospectors soon followed. Within months the trickle metamorphosed into a continuous line of fortune seekers and adventurers.

Thus, there is no telling how many prospectors labored most of their lives hoping to see what Abe Lee saw when he peered into his pan on that frigid day in April 1860. Staring back at him was a black crescent of sand awash with sparkling gold flecks and nuggets. Instantly he knew he had struck it rich. Before firing four shots and building the signal fire, Lee reputedly shouted "I've just got California in this here pan!" His exultation became part of Leadville myth almost as soon as he hollered it (if, in fact, he did).

It is no myth, however, that by mid-summer of 1860 nearly 5,000 spirited and hardy fortune seekers poured into America's newest gold-field bonanza, overrunning Abe Lee's "California Gulch." Although originally called Bough Town, the conglomeration of tents and log cabins that soon lined the gulch eventually took for its name the Spanish word for gold: Oro City. The first woman to arrive in Oro City was Augusta Tabor, wife of a man from Vermont named Horace Austin Warner ("H.A.W.") Tabor, who set up a small general store to meet the needs of the miners pouring into the camp. Food and mining supplies were often more important than money. But the placer-gold feeding frenzy did not last long. In less than five years a mass of miners had stripped the placer claims of their precious gold. By the mid-1860s, Oro City had dwindled to less than 500 souls. An early *Grip-Sack Guide of Colorado (1885)* read, ". . . California Gulch of 1859 [1860?], famous for its gold placer diggings, from which over $5,000,000 were taken, from date of discovery to 1864, when [they were] abandoned." Ever optimistic, the Tabors decided to remain.

In 1868 there was another short flurry of activity when the first underground gold mine, the Printer Boy, opened in California Gulch. By the mid-1870s the Printer Boy had closed and the miners who remained in this remote and primitive mountain region cursed the gritty black sand that

Hydraulic Mining in California Gulch in the Early Days.

Early miners in California Gulch pose for the photographer. (Author's collection: Unless noted otherwise, images are from the author's collection.)

H. A. W. Tabor was and still is
Leadville's most famous citizen.
(Courtesy of Barb Bost)

Augusta Tabor would not share the
same economic fate as her husband.
(Courtesy of Barb Bost)

clogged their sluices. The easy gold was long gone. Soon, it seemed, all the miners would be gone, too.

By 1875 there was still no Leadville, nor any indication that there would be. A few abandoned log cabins were scattered throughout the area, silent witnesses to nearby California Gulch's boom and bust in the early 1860s. Like those before them, the few miners who remained cursed the black sand that clogged the ripples in their sluice boxes. It seemed like all they could earn for their trouble was pocket change. Then one day in 1876, according to most accounts, less than a mile from Abe Lee's famous discovery in California Gulch, a couple of recalcitrant miners, William H. Stevens and Alvinus B. Wood, decided — for whatever reason — to have the abominable black sand assayed. When the report came back, they must have been momentarily dumbfounded, then ecstatic. The "cursed black sand" was lead carbonate, brimming with silver! For over a year they kept their secret, unobtrusively buying defunct gold claims along the seven-mile-long California Gulch. According to some historians, when Stevens and Wood hired more miners to help them work their claims, their secret became known. Once the word of the silver strike got out in early 1877, it spread like wildfire throughout Colorado, and beyond.

By late 1877 the rush was on. It proved to be one of the richest, longest-lived, bawdiest phenomenon that America has ever witnessed. The vortex of this massive rush was soon dubbed "Leadville" after the lead carbonate which bore its fortunes. During the last three years of the 1870s, the hyperboles freely invoked by editorial pundits to describe this "New Eldorado" could hardly live up to the reality they meant to describe.

If one were to believe the magazine and newspaper accounts, finding silver near Leadville, first known as Carbonate Camp, was relatively easy. Imagine hearing the following yarn — never mind that tales of fabulous chance discoveries involving deer surfaced in most early mining camps. Early Leadville's version involved the Long brothers and their partner, Charles Derry. The story goes that in September 1876, Jacob Long shot a deer along the divide between Iowa and Empire Gulches. Before the deer died it kicked a black rock which Long noticed and brought back to camp. He figured it was coal and so tossed it on the fire. Then, before the Long's and Derry's eyes, it metamorphosed into a molten mass of silver carbonate. To this day the knoll where the deer "kicked up a fortune" retains the name "Long and Derry Hill." As for "easy silver," *Scribner's Monthly* (October 1879) reported, "Prospectors went everywhere seeking for carbonates, radiating from this center up all the gulches, and over the foothills, delving almost anywhere at a venture. One day, at a hitherto unheard-of-point, wealth comes up by the bucketful out of the deep narrow hole, that has been pierced unostentatiously."

An early photograph—taken in the vicinity of what would become the world-renown Leadville Mining District — captures the essence of an isolated prospector's life before thousands of fortune seekers overran the region.

Freighters struggle up Mosquito Pass in 1879. (Reprinted from Frank Leslie's Illustrated Newspaper, *April 12, 1879)*

In the late 1870s the main jumping-off point to Leadville was Denver. To reach Leadville (dubbed Cloud City) from Denver, many people chose to negotiate the 13,000-foot Mosquito Pass — impossible in the winter and what life insurance companies called "extra hazardous" in the summer. Hauling heavy equipment over the treacherous trail exacted a terrible toll on animals and men (Flynn, 1959). Nevertheless, soon Mosquito Pass "that but a year before had been almost desolate in its loneliness, was lined with a straggling stream of humanity, with their faces set toward the new *El Dorado* [sic] (*Frank Leslie's Illustrated Newspaper*, April 12, 1879). Captain Robert G. Dill, editor of the *Herald Democrat*, observed that in 1878 almost every freight team available in Denver "was pressed into service" for Leadville. "Freighters demanded and obtained their own rates: 4, 5, 6, and even 10 cents a pound were not infrequently paid for wagon freight from Denver, and one instance is recorded, in which 25 cents per pound was paid for a wagon load of liquor, then an absolute necessity — so considered — in the new camp."

As for food, by 1878 "market hunters" scoured the adjacent hills in search of wild game. Frank H. Mayer, one such hunter, wrote in his diary (Roth, 1963) on August 18, 1878:

A record kill during the past week: twenty-four deer, twenty-two ante-lope, nine elk, five mountain sheep and a big silvertip bear. Woods [his partner] had to make two trips to take them out. I believe I am getting a bit sated with all this killing. It has lost all pleasure for me and I believe I will quit when rutting season opens. It has now degenerated into hard work with no thrills, a purely mechanical process . . . find the game, kill it, and then sweat to get it out.

Denver newspapers and the railroads "advertised the camp in exaggerated praise all over the East for the sake of patronage; and many an uneasy ne'er-do-well, and energetic prospector, and greedy saloonkeeper, and many a businessman who wanted to profit by the foolishness or necessity of the rest, started for Leadville" (*Frank Leslie's Illustrated Newspaper*, April 12, 1879). Leadville's population soared from a few hundred people in 1877 to over 10,000, some say 18,000, by the summer of 1879. It was like a huge metropolis suddenly appeared at an altitude of over 10,000 feet between two massive mountain ranges where there had been nothing only two years earlier. Plus, it was tough, especially in winter, to get there. On July 5, 1879, *Frank Leslie's Illustrated Newspaper*, a popular nationwide publication, exclaimed:

The city of Leadville is one of the marvels of the present age. Two years ago it had no existence, while today it has its long streets and

An artist sketched this overview of Leadville in 1879. (Reprinted from Frank Leslie's Illustrated Newspaper, July 5, 1879)

broad avenues many miles in extent, with large and handsome buildings on every side. Recently as August, 1877, only six rude log cabins were to be found, where to-day well designed edifices can be counted by the thousand.

In the 1870s, Leadville also experienced a libidinal release seldom seen even in the most decadent frontier boom towns. Many contemporaries roundly condemned Leadville as a den of iniquity and a pestilence that bowed only before its demigods: sex, liquor, gambling, and avarice. Others lavishly praised the Cloud City as being a living monument to the American Dream, where anyone, either through hard work or pure luck, could become fabulously rich. Based on the thousands of eager immigrants from throughout the United States and Europe who flocked to Leadville, one might conclude that there was merit in both views.

The 1879 *Leadville City Directory* listed, among numerous other business enterprises, 10 dry goods stores, 4 churches, 4 banks, 31 restaurants, 120 saloons, 19 beer halls, and 118 gambling houses and private clubs. Surveyors, of course, were in great demand. An honest one could earn a lot of money quickly. A dishonest one could earn even more. The same could be said for assayers. Claim jumping also proved to be rampant. Thus, over seventy lawyers and law firms also advertised in the 1879 *Leadville City Directory.*

***A mass of fortune seekers, horses, and wagons clogged Chestnut Street.
(Reprinted from** Frank Leslie's Illustrated Newspaper, April 12, 1879.)*

Poker and booze around the clock attracted hard-working miners as well as less savory characters. (Reprinted from Frank Leslie's Illustrated Newspaper, April 26, 1879)

Carlyle C. Davis, with his total available capital of $1,000, managed to publish the first edition of the first daily newspaper in the booming camp. A single twenty-foot by thirty-foot room served as his headquarters for his editorial, business, composing, job, and press departments, plus sleeping accommodations for eighteen men. The first edition of the *Daily Chronicle* hit the streets on January 29, 1879. So great was the demand that the news-hungry residents of the camp competed to buy the newspaper well into the evening hours.

As for the pace of life, one early Leadville pilgrim effused, "You can possibly have no idea of the rapidity of action here. All is push and bustle. The streets are crowded and every other house is a saloon, dance house, etc. I am writing now in the shadow of seven bottles of some odoriferous substance" (quoted in Blair, 1980). Edward Blair, one of Leadville's finest historians, also quoted a first-time visitor, "We could look up its [Chestnut Street] length, possible [sic] two miles. It was a crawling mass of horses, mules, wagons, and men. It looked impossible to get through, but we made it in about two hours."

As for the health of its new citizenry, the editor of the *Herald Democrat* lamented, "During the first year of Leadville's existence, it was almost universally regarded as an absolute death trap" (Dill, 1881). He felt this reputation, however, was undeserved, "It is well understood that a man who took care of himself and avoided exposure and excessive use of intoxicants, was in no greater danger than in the healthiest localities of the East."

Bawdy State Street, origin of many maladies, was the home of Leadville's notorious red light and gaming district. Of Leadville's morals, or lack thereof, Duane Smith, perhaps Colorado's finest historian, noted that Leadville "was the only camp which seemed to take pride in its depravity" (1989). One eyewitness observed, "The theatres, twirling casinos, the concert halls, the silver exchanges, and the A-lafranzanzas are all Argus-eyed and aglow. Down State Street a female voice is singing murder. Struggling up Harrison Avenue is a band of carousals singing something about not going home until mor-horning." Yet the eyewitness contended that it was worse two months prior. "Then guns were firing all along the line. Now one can stand on a street corner twenty minutes without hearing the whiz of a single bullet. Alas! Alas!" (quoted in Irey, 1951).

Of the sordid State Street, Blair (1980) lamented:

> The lowest rung on the social ladder was crowded with an army of variously painted and gowned harlots. There were those who haunted the saloons, dance halls, and cribs on State Street and those who ran the 'fancy houses' on West Third and West Fifth Streets . . . . The number of bodies of men, women, and children in Stillborn Alley, especially unwanted infants born of the wretches who inhabited the cribs along State Street surely gave the alley its name.

Leadville's distinctive Church of the Annunciation still stands.

On the other end of the moral continuum, Leadville, soon to be the second largest city in the new State of Colorado, justifiably pointed to its lofty Church of Annunciation. Father Henry Robinson was responsible for starting the first Catholic Church in Lake County. He had been appointed to the mission at Fairplay and all other camps along the Arkansas River in 1875. After he moved to Leadville in the late 1870s he raised funds to build the present brick church on the corner of East Seventh and Poplar Streets. To this day this striking edifice beckons the faithful. The "Unsinkable Molly Brown" of *Titanic* fame took her marriage vows there in 1886. In

1935 a funeral mass for Elizabeth Bonduel "Baby Doe" Tabor took place in its confines.

Civic-minded Leadvillites also spearheaded the construction of the magnificent Lake County Courthouse and agreed to pay a "professional," if not overly aggressive, police force. The first hospital to be erected was St. Vincent's. Soon after its opening in 1878, patients filled it to capacity. By 1879 people were standing in lines for hours to receive mail at the new Leadville Post Office. Mail meant a cherished word from home, lover, or perhaps a business associate. For many early Leadvillites it was their only personal contact with the outside world.

Lake County's magnificent courthouse graced Harrison Avenue for over five decades.

Denizens of early Leadville frequently crowded their new post office. (Reprinted from Leslie's Illustrated Newspaper, *May 3, 1879)*

As early as 1878, Leadville's citizenry had demonstrated a concern over the probability of fire. Even a spark in this warren of hastily built wooden structures could ignite a fiery Armageddon. Indeed, since its inception in 1878, Leadville, like other early Colorado mining towns, was an explosion waiting to happen. These worries led to the establishment — as was the practice in other newly born cities and boom towns — of a volunteer fire company.

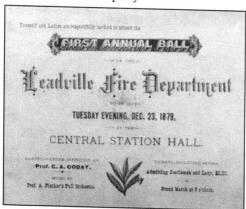

Only those who moved in certain social circles received this cherished invitation to Leadville's "First Annual Ball," sponsored by the Leadville Fire Department.

Volunteer fire squads were an integral part of Leadville and its citizens, and were supported to some degree by both. Mostly, however, early fire companies depended on volunteers' donations of time, effort, and even funds. Despite instances of drunken shenanigans (not peculiar, it must be said, to Leadville) such fire brigades grew into sources of immense community pride. They stood as pillars of defense against the ever-present danger of a cataclysmic conflagration, and additionally some of the town's social activities centered around the dashing, daring, and handsome fire laddies.

In May 1879, it almost happened. From the north a forest fire crept toward the city, spreading as it approached and threatening to encircle the town. Several outlying cabins were quickly devoured, and Mayor William H. James called out the volunteer firefighters as well as all citizens to cut fire lanes, trenches, and build backfires. As the flames lapped at the city's edge, the wind direction changed and Leadville was saved.

As a direct result of this scare, the city installed a fire hydrant and alarm system. Leadville desperately needed pressurized water as well as a method of locating fires quickly. By December 8, 1879, Leadville had both: seventeen hydrants were in place throughout the city and a fire tower — with bell — was erected near the city center.

In its excitement, however, Leadville must have forgotten how high and cold the city could be, because the hydrants froze in winter. "Four out of five plugs frozen, and the other one-fifth freezing [rapidly]," reported the *Herald Democrat* on January 29, 1880. By the time the council stopped bickering over who was responsible for the poor planning, the ground was frozen too deep and the snow piled too high to rebury the pipes. So the volunteers suffered through a miserable winter, trying — with little success — to keep the fire plugs thawed. By the next summer, the pipes were lowered to a safe level.

The celebrated fire bell, meantime, became so brittle in the bitter cold that the fire laddies dared not ring it, fearing it would crack and fall apart. They had to man the fire tower throughout the winter in an attempt to spot fires before they spread.

Thanks to a common man with the Midas touch, Horace Tabor, nascent Leadville soon boasted a magnificent opera house, truly a high-culture edifice. Completed in 1879, the Tabor Opera House's opening night "was marred by a recent vigilante hanging across the street" (Irey, 1951). Although heralded to be the best opera house between St. Louis and San Francisco, it shared the stage with at least five other "theatres" in Leadville. For a while, most of them proved profitable. The Theatre Comique, "a 50' by 100' wooden structure, rented for $1,700 per month or $20,400 per year and still made a profit, the estimated gross daily receipts being $1,200" (Irey, 1951).

In 1882, the famous and infamous English dandy, Oscar Wilde, delivered a lecture on beauty and his aesthetic movement to a surprisingly receptive and respectful audience at the Tabor Opera House. After the lecture, Horace Tabor, who attended the performance, escorted Wilde to the Matchless Mine. Oscar was lowered by bucket into a new shaft named for him, "The Oscar." At the bottom of the shaft a gourmet meal pleased all who partook. Wilde chatted with the miners and observed

One of the West's architectural treasures, the Tabor Opera House, is now open to the public. (Denver Public Library, Western History Department)

them working most of the night, going straight from the Matchless to his 4:30 a.m. train.

As for sleeping accommodations, "In Leadville, there were not sleeping accommodations for those who thronged into the camp. For the privilege of lying on a dirty mattress, laid upon the floor of a boarding tent, with a suspicious blanket for a cover, and the chances of proximity to a thief or a desperado, those who could afford it paid a dollar" (Dill, 1881). By 1879, however, William Bush, who later would become entangled with Horace Tabor's infamous divorce from his first wife, Augusta, financed the construction of Leadville's only first-class hotel. It "opened for business at 302-306 Harrison Avenue on April 10, 1879. It immediately attracted prominent mining men and capitalists along with governmental representations. In fact, the three-story building was so popular that it paid for itself within 30 days. The main dining room was 24 feet by 54 feet with a 12-foot high ceiling" (*Herald Democrat*, 1981). A walkway connected the Clarendon to the third floor of the Tabor Opera House.

It is no surprise that in early Leadville money was the business to be in. "Leadville . . . was a retail merchant's dream. Everyone consumed, was willing to pay the price, and, for the most part, could afford to pay the price" (Blair, 1980). To wit, a good merchandise store could earn up to $40,000 — a small fortune in the 1870s — in one month. Banks sprung up like wildflowers. Tabor built a bank on the corner of Chestnut Street and Harrison Avenue. The First National Bank "erected a handsome stone building on Harrison Avenue . . . setting an example which was speedily

To this day Harrison Avenue remains Leadville's main street.

followed, and the city began to assume metropolitan airs in the number and character of other buildings, as well as the throngs of people that crowded the streets" (Dill, 1881). Yet there was no mention of the log cabin that stubbornly remained in the middle of Harrison Avenue, "main street of American mining" (Dill, 1881).

And mining is what Leadville was all about. By the end of the 1870s, over seventy major mines and mining companies pumped the life's blood into Leadville bulging veins. Leadville could never have been, well, Leadville, without the mines. While shopkeepers hawked their goods, State Street plied its trade, lawyers argued, carpenters constructed, men drank, women socialized, the faithful worshiped, doctors ministered to the needs of the sick and injured — of which there were plenty, and miners kept digging deeper. Spectacularly rich veins, lucky strikes, and near-mythical characters ushered in the boom years of the 1880s.

Mines and miners constituted the backbone of Leadville's dizzying success. Shown here is the Louisville Mine and its miners. (Left: Lake County Public Library, Colorado Mountain History Collection)

CHAPTER TWO

Boom Days and The Tabors (1880s)

During this decade the eyes of the United States and Europe often looked toward Leadville. This was no surprise, since the two-mile-high city — with its population rapidly approaching 25,000 (some say 40,000) — reigned in almost every form of excess, including the extremely profitable silver-mining industry.

Prospectors, like Abe Lee almost two decades earlier, repeatedly started the money train rolling. In 1878, George R. Fryer, "a bull-headed man, though kindly, with little or no regard for experts, real or otherwise . . . . decided there was silver in the small hills to the north of the boom area" (Blair, 1980). Fryer lived with his partner, John Borden, in a primitive log cabin. They prospected alone, digging shallow holes randomly. One day Fryer hit good ore. In less than two months this unassuming knoll became known as Fryer's Hill. It also became the most expensive real estate in the world. Fryer, like Borden, did not have enough money to develop the mine, which he named the New Discovery, so he sold out for a reported $50,000 to Jerome B. Chaffee, Colorado's first Senator and business magnate. Chicken Hill, Carbonate Hill, Stray Horse Gulch, Jonny Hill, Breece Hill, Lee Basin, Evans Gulch, Iowa Gulch, California Gulch, and many more carried similar stories of chance discoveries and fortunes changing hands.

No individual in Leadville's storied history, however, proved to be more lucky, acquire more fame, and amass more wealth than Horace Austin Warner ("H.A.W.") Tabor, and he wasn't even a prospector. Horace and his wife, Augusta, and their son, Maxie, arrived in California Gulch (Oro City) in 1860 to set up a small general store. Seldom did Tabor prospect, although many a prospector — too many according to Augusta — received a grubstake from the affable storeowner. Grubstaking was a common practice in early mining camps. Storeowners outfitted prospectors with tools, food, and sometimes mules in exchange for a promise of a portion of the profits — if they hit pay dirt. While in Oro City, Tabor never grubstaked the right prospector.

After the placer gold and most of the people disappeared from Oro City, the Tabors stayed in the region. Over the years they set up shop in Buckskin Joe and Malta, then moved all their stock to a store in Leadville when the silver rush started in the late 1870s. The generous and likeable Tabor became Leadville's first mayor and second postmaster, comfortably settling into his new home and position of social influence. He also loved to gamble, apparently with some success, as well as spend long hours visiting with the boys. Augusta often tended the store. When Tabor kept shop he continued his practice of subsidizing prospectors, with no luck.

Then on April 15, 1878, as Tabor later recalled, two German immigrants, August Rische and George Hook, ambled into his store seeking a grubstake. Tabor also remembered that there was nothing exceptional about this twosome. Worse, they actually wanted to prospect near Fryer's discovery, which most locals, including Tabor, considered a geological anomaly. Nevertheless, Tabor gave the men tools, enough food for a week, and, supposedly, a jug of whiskey in exchange for one-third interest in all their "findings." The rest, as they say, is history.

The two Germans found their bonanza exactly where the geological experts said it could not be — near Fryer's Hill. They named it the Little Pittsburg, without the "h" because the proper spelling had been used for another claim, after Hook's hometown. At first Tabor helped them work their claim. By fall of 1878 each of the three partners took out $10,000 in profit. Soon Hook, who was not enamored with Leadville, sold out to Rische and Tabor. Later Rische sold out to David Moffat and Horace Tabor for a mindboggling $265,500. From then on it seemed like every property Tabor purchased — from the Little Pittsburg to the Matchless — brought him yet another fortune. Consider this: at one point the Little Pittsburg was producing $8,000 to $10,000 a *day*. The Matchless Mine, named after a popular brand of chewing tobacco, paid Tabor on average $2,000 a *day*. Plus, Tabor sold out his share of the Little Pittsburg for exactly one million dollars, just before it stopped producing such rich silver ore in early 1880. And there were no taxes.

RUINS OF THE FAMOUS (TABOR) MATCHLESS MINE   W-1205

Of the hundreds of mines in the Leadville region, none became more famous than the Matchless.

Just east of the Matchless, George Belt and William Knight discovere
what would become the richest of all the Fryer Hill properties. They name
it the Robert E. Lee. After it had been bought and sold a few times, its ric
silver chloride once paid $250,000 in one month. As if this was not enough
during one seventeen hour period it yielded an astonishing $118,000.

Such astronomical financial successes attracted worldwide attentior
luring even more fortune seekers to Leadville. The vast majority wer
keenly disappointed. The truth is, as previously mentioned, very fev
prospectors ever struck it rich in Leadville, the rest of Colorado, or any
where else in the West. Bankers, stockbrokers (mostly Eastern), lawyers
hotel owners, doctors, saloonkeepers, and storeowners usually fared bette
financially than prospectors, and certainly hired miners. Yet abysmal odd
never seemed to faze the glassy-eyed hordes of money-hungry pilgrims
Moreover, even if prospectors discovered a rich mineral deposit, it woul
not have made them rich. Having the Midas touch, like Fryer, Rische, o
Hook, was not enough. It took thousands of dollars in labor and capital t
extract precious mineral from the ore in which it was embedded. Before
prospector saw a dime, unless someone came along and bought his claim
his ore had to be mined, transported to a smelter (a daunting, expensiv
task in mountainous terrain), crushed, refined, melted into bullion, anc
sent off to buyers hundreds, sometimes thousands, of miles away. Most o
the starry-eyed fortune seekers would have done better financially b
staying home, no matter how meager their income.

Mining history seldom gives smelters their due, perhaps because of th
dismal working conditions and their foul by-products. But without th
droning belching smelters, Leadville would not have continued to thrive
"Wonderfully successful, it is through them [the smelters], more than an
one agency, that the City itself owes its present size and importance. Th
most prominent works are those of the Grant Smelting Company" (Dill
1881). By 1880, Grant Smelting "operated seven large stacks" and had pro
duced more that "$4,000,000 worth of bullion" (Dill, 1881). In fact
Leadville became the smelting center of Colorado with twenty-one smelter
in the 1880s. Without them, Leadville and the entire Colorado minin
industry would not have been as productive. In 1883 alone, these smelter
had on hand approximately 100,000 tons of Leadville ore. By 1883, th
Harrison Reduction Works, among others, helped produce 179,000 tons o
lead, 35,250 ounces of silver, and 50,000 ounces of gold. The Harrison
Reduction Works's massive slag dump, until recently, loomed over th
southern end of Harrison Avenue. (Today many historically inclined local
lament its removal by the Environmental Protection Agency.)

In 1878, August R. Meyer, who later became part owner of the Arkansas
Valley Smelting Company, built a home for his bride which, for a time, wa

GRANT SMELTER. LEADVILLE.

Leadville would not have prospered without smelters like this one.

Although smelters helped Leadville's economy, they spewed toxic wastes into the earth and sky. Shown here is the Arkansas Valley Smelter, one of several operating at full capacity during the boom days.

the envy of all Leadville. August and his wife, Emma, furnished their home in elaborate Victorian style. Frequent visits by Leadville's prominent citizens made it a center of social activity. In 1881 Daniel Healy purchased the home and leased it as a boardinghouse from 1897 to 1902. To accommodate more boarders, most of them schoolteachers, a third story was added in 1898. Today the house, called the Healy House, is owned by the Colorado Historical Society and operates as a public museum. Astute businessman James V. Dexter's 1879 rough-hewn log cabin, constructed a year later than the Healy House, sits on the museum property and is also open to the public. Visitors are surprised by what they find inside the abode's crude exterior.

Astride California Gulch were the A. Y. and Minnie Mines. Neither produced for years. Then in 1880 a Jewish immigrant from Pennsylvania, named Meyer Guggenheim, purchased them with Charles Graham for $4,000. Profits the next month soared to $17,231. The unexpected bonanza, combined with wise investments in the smelting industry, propelled the Guggenheims to their vast fortune.

The first "Iron Horse," the most efficient and modern mode of transportation during this era, arrived in Leadville on July 22, 1880. It signaled the start of a sustained economic boom, the likes of which Leadville has been searching for ever since. More people, supplies, and mining equipment rode behind the smoke-and-cinder spewing engines that chugged

This is not an early version of The Little Engine That Could. *Rather, it is an early illustration of the South Park chugging up Kenosha Pass on its way to the boom town of boom towns — Leadville.*

Only occasionally did fierce winter storms — and there were plenty — stop the trains to the two-mile-high boom town.

their way into the mountains. More bullion, tons and tons of it, could be shipped out faster and more efficiently as well.

Even though it was close to midnight when the first Denver & Rio Grande train pulled into the new depot, the occasion sparked a tumultuous celebration. Small wonder, for not only did the arrival of the narrow-gauge railroad promise even more economic prosperity, it carried General and Mrs. Ulysses Grant and their considerable entourage into the Cloud City for a "frantic five-day visit, part of their round-the-world tour" (Blair, 1980). The excitement on that late night in July was almost too much, even for Leadville.

Construction of a railroad through mountainous terrain was an expensive and Herculean task. That did not, however, deter other railroad companies, and competition among railroads serving Leadville became fierce. Soon came a second narrow-gauge railroad, the Denver, South Park & Pacific that had an agreement to rent the Denver & Rio Grande's track from Buena Vista to Leadville.

On August 8, 1880, the *Leadville Chronicle* noted that, "So rushing is the freight business of both companies that large numbers of cars are on tracks and have been there several days awaiting their turn to be unloaded." By 1885 it cost Denver & Rio Grande passengers $12.95 to travel the mountainous 151 miles from Denver to Leadville — far faster and safer than trudging over treacherous Mosquito Pass. The Denver & Rio Grande's main competitor, the Union Pacific (who purchased the Denver, South Park & Pacific), charged the same.

In 1886, the Denver & Rio Grande Railroad, which had become dominant, did not take the proposed Colorado Midland Railway seriously. It should have. The standard-gauge Midland — a first for the Colorado mountains — arrived in Leadville in 1887 (a cloudburst sent the 3,000 spectators scrambling for cover) and gave the Denver & Rio Grande stiff competition for many years.

Of course dreams of wealth, most of which fast disappeared, combined with the need to find lodging, food, and an affordable grubstake, preoccupied most of the eager fortune seekers who disembarked at one of the new train stations every day of the week in the early 1880s. Many of them came to Leadville just to be part of the action. Among those who stepped off the trains were Margaret Tobin (before she became Margaret "Molly" Brown), John Henry (Doc) Holliday, Tom Horn, Wyatt Earp, Bat Masterson, and the Daltons, plus scores of famous actors, writers, poets, and politicians, including presidents of the United States. In fact, it seemed like everyone came to Leadville. Yet none of them could rival, at least in local notoriety, Leadville's legendary lovers, Horace Austin Warner Tabor and Elizabeth Bonduel McCourt Doe. The highly public and tangled web of passion, riches, and misfortune spun by the "Silver King" and his young lover "Baby Doe," ultimately contained all the elements of a classical Greek tragedy.

Elizabeth Bonduel McCourt was born in Oshkosh, Wisconsin. She married a local boy, Harvey Doe, on June 27, 1877. That same year they moved

Colorado Midland construction workers needed refreshments, too. (Courtesy of Bruce and Hillery McCalister)

to the golden hills of Central City, Colorado. In 1879 she divorced Harvey Doe, then traveled to Leadville. There her extraordinary beauty and charisma caught the attention of, by now, one of the most powerful and wealthy men in the West: Horace Tabor. Tabor found her charms irresistible.

Women of "good social standing" rallied to Augusta Tabor's side. It did no good. Horace's infatuation with the youthful Elizabeth only intensified. One day in 1881 Augusta's husband of twenty-three years moved out. Still, she would not grant him a divorce. Frustrated, Horace asked William H. Bush, his trusted associate, to secure a divorce secretly. Unbeknownst to Tabor, Bush botched the divorce. Soon thereafter, on September 30, 1882, Horace secretly married — or so he thought — Elizabeth Bonduel McCourt Doe, who has come to be known throughout the world as Baby Doe Tabor. Later, Tabor's first marriage to Elizabeth McCourt Doe was ruled illegal.

Finally, the asocial Augusta reluctantly granted Horace a legal divorce, but not for free. In a legal "Complaint for Alimony" (Cassidy, undated) filed on April 1, 1882, Augusta L. Tabor's lawyer stated, "That on or about

Shown here is the young woman, Elizabeth Bonduel McCourt Doe, who came to Leadville, caught the eye of one of the richest men in the West, and became a Leadville legend. (Courtesy of Barb Bost)

the month of Jan. 1881 the said defendant [H. A. W. Tabor] . . . willfully deserted and absented himself from said plaintiff, and ever since has and continues willfully and without cause to desert and abandon said plaintiff and to live separate and apart from her without any sufficient cause or for any lawful reason and against her wish, will and consent."

The lawyer continued, "That shortly after their marriage the defendant and plaintiff removed to the then territory, now the State of Kansas, and thence in the year 1859 to Colorado; that by their common mutual exertions, patient industry and economy for more than twenty-three years they acquired a property, real, mineral and personal, a partial and imperfect description of which is set forth herein and is believed to be approximately correct . . . . to wit:

> *The Tabor Opera House block $800,000*
> *The Tabor Block $250,000*
> *Block 3 Brown's Addition $100,000*
> *Dwelling on Welton St. $20,000*
> *8 lots Block 98 East Denver $100,000*
> *4 lots Block 107 East Denver $100,000*
> *97 shares First National Bank $500,000*
> *Bush Building, Leadville $30,000*
> *Coliseum Theatre Leadville $20,000*
> *Bank in Gunnison City $70,000*
> *Gas stock and loan to company $100,000*
> *Matchless Mine $1,000,000*
> *Tabor mill and telephone stock $75,000*
> *Bank of Leadville capital and profits $100,000*
> *Henrietta, Maid of Erin, Waterlook mines $1,000,000*
> *Breece-Iron $300,000*
> *Chrysolite $50,000*
> *Glass-Pendary $100,000*
> *Smuggler, Lead Chief, and Denver City mines $500,000*
> *Interest in Bull Domingo and Robinson $100,000*
> *Polite and group $100,000*
> *Mines in Summit County $100,000*
> *Interest in Fibse Manufacturing Co. Old Mexico $50,000*
> *Investment in lands and mortgage bonds near Chicago $500,000*
> *275 acres of land near stockyards in Chicago $50,000*
> *Lands in Kansas, Colorado lands in South Park, railroad stocks,*
> *   shares in Denver Steam Heating Co., Durango stage line $120,000*
> *Government bonds $200,000*
> *23/48 Tam O'Shanter mine $100,000*
> *Moneys, loans, stocks, etc. $200,000*
> *Diamonds and other jewels $100,000*
> *Denver Utah and Pacific Construction Co. $100,000*
> *Hibernia $100,000*

"The whole said property being of the estimated value of about $9 million," (Cassidy, M., undated) of which Augusta ultimately received "$300,000 in property" (Smith, 1989).

In 1881 Dill, early Leadville historian and editor of the *Herald Democrat*, praised Tabor, "Strange as it may seem, he made no mistakes, but coined 'a mint of money' with every deal. Like the fabled Midas, everything he touched seemed to turn to gold." So it went until Tabor, a newly appointed United States Senator, married — this time legally — Elizabeth McCourt in Washington, D. C., on March 1, 1883. Most women shunned this "sordid affair," but several prominent politicians, including President Chester A. Arthur, stopped by to wish them well.

Horace showered his young blond bride with extravagant gifts, including a $75,000 diamond necklace. Colorado U. S. Senator Henry Teller, whom Tabor briefly replaced in the Senate after Teller was appointed Secretary of the Interior, said of the wedding, ". . . Tabor is an honest man in money affairs, and I believe he

H.A.W. Tabor's stunning young bride, "Baby Doe Tabor," poses for a photographer. (Courtesy of Barb Bost)

Here Lily Tabor, Elizabeth Tabor's beautiful first-born, "Age 24 Months," poses regally for the photographers.

Perhaps it was best that Elizabeth Tabor's second-born, Silver Dollar, "Age 14 Weeks," could not see into her future.

is truthful, but he has made a great fool of himself with reference to that woman . . . ." (quoted in Smith, 1989).

In 1886 Margaret Tobin, like many women before her, came to Leadville not to mine, but to find a rich husband. She moved in with her brother Daniel, who worked as a miner for the going rate of $2.50 a day. Daniels, Fisher, & Smith hired Margaret to sew carpets and draperies. Although she intended to marry a wealthy man, enabling her to care for her family back in Hannibal, Missouri, she soon discovered, like in most cities, that there was a paucity of wealthy men. At a church picnic during the summer of 1886 she met James Joseph "J. J." Brown, the ambitious and experienced foreman of the Louisville Mine (see page 15). He was not a rich man. Several years after he married Margaret, Brown became wealthy. He developed new mining techniques as well as discovered a rich body of gold ore in the bowels of the Ibex Mining Complex (formerly the Little Jonny). Out of appreciation for Brown's extraordinary efforts and discovery, the owners of the Ibex gave him 12,500 shares, or one-eight interest, in the immensely lucrative mining complex. Brown's financial ship had come in. "Maggie," as she preferred to be called by her friends, would not have responded to "Molly," a moniker bestowed upon her by Hollywood writers many years after her death.

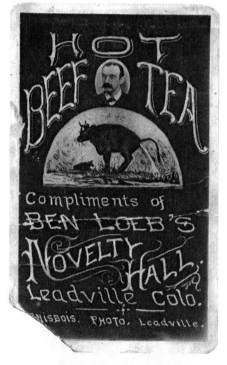

By 1886, Leadville boasted several more hotels to accommodate the hundreds of guests who arrived almost daily. Commercial building also thrived. Three brothers from Delaware built the three-story brick Delaware Block on Harrison Avenue and Seventh Street. Stores occupied the lower floor while office space and rooms "rented by the month" filled the upper two floors. In 1890, the lower floor became the R. H. Beggs and Company Dry Goods store. Twelve years later the new owners changed the name to the Crews-Beggs Trading Company. Since 1992, this venerable establishment, now a hotel, has allowed visitors to experience Leadville's past glory in its beautifully renovated confines.

Ben Loeb excelled at wickedness which was in great demand in early Leadville.

During the 1880s, over a hundred saloons, gambling halls, and "bawdy houses" were as much a part of Leadville as the mining business. Ben Loeb was one of the most successful entrepreneurs on the seamy side. Brass band members often distributed flyers for Ben Loeb's "Concert, Sporting, and Novelty Hall" in front of his establishment. Most of the added attractions in Loeb's place were also come-ons for the prostitutes, commonly called "soiled doves" and "fallen angels." On January 22, 1912, the *Carbonate Weekly Chronicle* published a lengthy obituary for Benjamin Loeb. It began:

> *After a life connected with merry making of the wildest sort and with display of the most spectacular kind, after winning the name of being one of the striking figures of the early days, Ben Loeb died yesterday afternoon . . . . At one time his name was the more frequently heard on the streets of Leadville than that of any other person in camp.*

Thus, while female company could be had for a price, lasting companionship for young men in Leadville was hard to find. The 1880 census counted 15,185 people, only 3,794 of whom were female.

Ironically, untamed Leadville provided an opportunity for women to enter new professions. Many became teachers, printers, bookkeepers, clerks, prospectors, and doctors. One reporter for the *Herald Democrat* went so far as to assert that, "Women have as a rule shown far greater perseverance in prosecuting prospect and exploration work than men."

The message on this advertising trade-token mirror was clear even to the illiterate. (Photograph by M. S. Strain)

Already a noted artist when she arrived in Leadville, Mary Hallock Foote became a writer, too. Within years the multitalented Foote earned a reputation as one of the best authors in the West.

In the 1880s several women doctors practiced medicine in Leadville as well, most specializing in women's health or pediatrics.

For the education and cultural enlightenment of the children, by 1880 "there were twelve schools in successful operation, with thirteen teachers" (Dill, 1881).

> *Going to school for a child in the early boom years in Leadville must have been an experience unequaled anywhere. Mothers whose children went to Central School gave long lectures about the evils of State Street and instructed their young to look neither right nor left and not to speak to anyone. Young boys and girls found themselves*

walking to and from school in ethnic neighborhoods where their ability to fight or flee was a necessity (Blair, 1980).

In the fall of 1880, "the first school of importance was commenced." Completed in 1881, it was praised as a "model in every respect. It occupied half a city block on Spruce Street . . . and is finished in a style fully equal to that of Denver schools" (Dill, 1881). In fact, Central School had gas lights and a telephone, but neither running water nor toilets.

The interior of this classroom and the apparel of the young students does not seem to reflect the wealth that was pouring out of the nearby mines. (Lake County Public Library, Colorado Mountain History Collection)

Churches, too, began to spring up in the better parts of the city. "Those who consider Leadville the caldron in which wickedness of every description seeths [sic] and boils, without a single redeeming circumstance, have not taken into account the efforts of those noble men, ever to be found in the van of civilization, struggling with wickedness and earnest in the endeavors to ameliorate the condition of mankind" (Dill, 1881). One early "van of civilization" was the Presbyterian Church. Designed by Eugene Robitaille and dedicated on December 23, 1889, its unique Gothic-styled bell tower still graces Harrison Avenue.

During the boom decade the first block of West Fourth Street became known as "Millionaires' Row" because of the moneyed people who settled there. Shown on the opposite page is the "House with the Eye" that master carpenter Eugene Robitaille built to accommodate his bride in 1879. It still stands proudly at 127 West Fourth Street. Among the rich who lived along

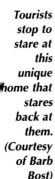

Tourists stop to stare at this unique home that stares back at them. (Courtesy of Barb Bost)

he affluent row were Dr. David H. Dougan, mayor and prominent businessman; A. V. Hunter, noted banker; and Joel W. Smith, manager of the Daniels and Fisher store whose Denver branch ultimately became the longstanding, successful business named May D & F.

Fishing and mining seem to be unlikely companions. Yet many miners loved to fish. So in 1889 Leadville landed a fish hatchery. The first eggs consisted of a collection of 568,000 brook trout eggs incubated in a temporary frame hatchery building during the fall of 1889. The first permanent Leadville National Fish Hatchery, constructed with native stone quarried near Basalt at a cost of $15,000, is the second oldest federal hatchery still operated by the Fish and Wildlife Service of the United States Department of the Interior. For decades it stocked rainbow, brook, and brown trout in waters which originally held only native cutthroat. Currently tours are available in and around the facility, which is located on the east side of Mount Massive at an elevation of over 10,000 feet.

In downtown Leadville, the volunteer firefighters kept a close watch for fires. Unfortunately, their firefighting behavior did not always meet the highest standards of professionalism. On May 19, 1882, a fire broke out at the corner of Harrison Avenue and East Chestnut Street, a major crossroads in downtown Leadville. In a matter of hours one square block was reduced to smoldering ruins, including the upscale Hotel Windsor. The total cost: $500,000 and at least one death. Only fireproof walls and the vaults of the First National Bank building kept the fire from spreading and, most likely, destroying the town.

Rumors abounded that members of one volunteer fire company had set the fire just to settle, once and for all, which was the fastest company! Even

if this proved to be a false rumor, no one could deny that the voluntee
actions during the fire were less than exemplary. While "several of th
firemen joked and kidded with members of the other companies," the fir
continued to smolder. One fire laddie went so far as to spray one of hi
friends in the crowd. When the potential seriousness of the blaze becam
apparent, every fireman in Leadville was summoned. Unfortunately, "man
who answered the call had been drinking for a considerable time . . .
(quoted in Blair, 1980).

*In the latter half of the 19th century, competition among fire departments
comprised the stuff of high drama. (Lake County Public Library, Colorado
Mountain History Collection)*

A newly elected Alderman, C. C. Joy, could not stand the sight of th
chaos at the Hotel Windsor fire. He screamed at the volunteers, callin
them "drunkin' sons of bitches," and accosted Andrew King, one of the ine
briated volunteers. Within three days the mayor and city council sum
marily passed an ordinance that terminated the services of the volunteer
and created a professional, paid department. Several of the hard-working
reliable volunteers were immediately hired.

Many of the major stockholders in the mines where absentee owner
who lived in financial centers back East. Most had little knowledge or con
cern about Leadville itself, as long as the mines kept producing. Many wh
became wealthy in Leadville, including Tabor, moved down to the mor
favorable climes and big-city amenities of Denver and towns back East.

Tabor's money and common-man personality landed him the lieutenant governor's position in Denver in 1878. While in Leadville and Denver, Tabor, who had a great sense of philanthropy, spent considerable amounts of his personal fortune on civil projects and community improvement — including magnificent opera houses in both cities and the building of the National Mining and Industrial Exposition in Denver in 1882. Tabor, like many other new movers and shakers, also wanted to put the West in control of its own destiny.

Throughout the 1880s, Leadville's sensational success fed on itself. In 1885, a popular guide to Colorado (*Crofutt's*) foretold nothing less than an economic Shangrila for the Cloud City:

> *Just as long as this work goes on, everything will be pushed forward by an irresistible force, and the Leadville of 1890 will be a city of 75,000 souls, producing annually a like amount in millions of gold, silver, and precious metals. The mines of Leadville and Colorado are practically inexhaustible, and were there no more discovered, those that are known to be rich and profitable to work, would require the labor of millions of hardy miners for many years to work out.*

With glowing reports such as these printed in the prospectuses, small wonder so many easterners gobbled up shares of stock in Leadville's mines. High dividends and astronomical appreciation seemed certain.

Over-worked and under-paid miners were the norm in Leadville and other mining cities throughout the West.

In spite of appearances and public perception, however, not everything went smoothly for Leadville during the boom decade. In fact, a wave of discontent swept through the miners' ranks as early as 1880. They were disgruntled for several reasons. First, difficult and dangerous working conditions prevailed in the mines. Second, many of the miners expected to own, not work in the mines. Third, they were paid only $2.50 to $3.50 a day. This seemed a pittance when compared with the mine owners' staggering profits. Finally, there were few, if any, benefits.

A general miners' strike was called in May 1880. It was a serious one, threatening the welfare of all Leadvillites. After protracted negotiations and even a declaration of martial law, the strike was settled on June 18. The owners won this battle, but there would be more to come.

During this exhilarating decade, no one seemed concerned about the implications of some discontented miners or a few mines "playing out." The rich mineral deposits in the earth below seemed inexhaustible. That the government of the United States of America continued a debate over its arcane silver-backed monetary system, and that some powerful Easterners kept clamoring for the repeal of the Silver Sherman Purchase Act, which had buoyed silver prices for years, did not seem to worry many Leadvillites, either. Why should they worry? They remained on an incredible trajectory of success that arched over adversity like a spectacular silver rainbow.

CHAPTER THREE

Silver Sinks, a Palace Melts, and Guns Roar (1890s)

The wheels of Leadville's mighty mining machine kept rolling in the early 1890s. Underground mining techniques had advanced well beyond the shovel, pick, hammer, and jack. Early air-drills could do the work of twenty men with single or double jacks in a fraction of the time. Better blasting caps ignited more potent explosives. More efficient and powerful machines pumped air into the tunnels and shafts as well as sucked water — a constant problem — out of them. Alternating-current electricity provided cheap, efficient power while safely illuminating the darkness in the depths. Buckets used to transport miners in and out of the deep mine shafts gave way to safer cages and small elevator platforms.

Mining activities now included downtown Leadville as well. "Ten shafts were [sunk] within the city limits of Leadville, opening up the Downtown district. Ore [was] encountered in Penrose, Gray, Eagle, Lazy Bill, and the Star of Hope shafts" (Emmons, Irving, and Loughlin, 1927). These mines, along with all the other mines in the vicinity, produced prodigious amounts of metal. Indeed, from 1879 to 1894 the total yield of silver (7,889,992 ounces), gold (96,712 ounces), lead (44,733,000 ounces), and zinc (270,000 ounces) amounted to almost $200,000,000.

If highgrading (smuggling out rich pieces of ore) were taken into account, some claim this amount would have been doubled.

Improved mining techniques quickly changed the face of underground mining.

Most miners justified stealing ore by comparing their meager financial recompense with the millions their owners received. Furthermore, few miners held any stock in the mines where they labored. Highgrading plagued small operations too, where no systematic searches for smuggled ore occurred. Consider the temptation: a tin lunch bucket stuffed with high-grade ore might bring more money than a month's worth of hard labor.

This is an unattributed photograph of one of the hundreds of small mines in the Leadville vicinity. The miner's dog seems excited about something. (Lake County Public Library, Colorado Mountain History Collection)

Suburbs sprouted above many of the rich ore deposits, especially east of the city. Some of them became independent settlements such as Adelaide, Alexander, Carbonate Hill, Evansville, Finntown, Howland, Oro City , Soda Springs, and Stumpftown. Combined with Leadville's burgeoning population, over 30,000 people now called the upper Arkansas Valley and surrounding foothills their home.

Residents could choose from among five newspapers (*Herald Democrat, Carbonate Chronicle, Leadville Evening Chronicle, Leadville Dispatch*, and the *Leadville Star*), three major railroads (Colorado Midland, Denver & Rio Grande, and the Union Pacific Railway), nine churches (First Baptist, Church of the Annunciation, Congregational, Temple Israel, First Evangelical Lutheran, First Methodist, Episcopal, St. George's, and the First Presbyterian), and nearly a hundred saloons — too numerous to list here, although the quantity suggests a high place on the list of the populace's priorities. Also available were wagon manufacturers, watchmakers, jewelers, tailors, steamship agencies, physicians, surgeons, photographers, restaurants, paper hangers, laundries, blacksmiths, meat markets, milliners,

Horse business was big business until the early 1900s. Wanklin and Peterson made carriages and shoed horses at 122 East Third Street. (Lake County Public Library, Colorado Mountain History Collection)

iveries, boot and shoe makers, and all other goods and services one might expect to find in a thriving city in America at the close of the 19th century (*Leadville City Directory, 1892*). Raucous and amoral activities still boomed on State Street, though most of these establishments did not appear in the city directories.

Leadville's animated social scene rivaled any in the West. (Before movies, television, VCRs, and the Internet, we are reminded that people provided most

Leadville's Drum Corps frequently performed for enthusiastic and appreciative audiences.

ANNUAL

Masquerade Ball

& Exhibition Drill

GIVEN BY THE

Leadville Drum Corps

AT CITY HALL,

Thanksgiving Eve, Wednesday, November 24, 1897.

of their own entertainment.) The Leadville Drum Corps and numerou
other musical organizations — from marching bands to orchestras –
attracted large and enthusiastic crowds. Famous Thespian companies, acro
batic groups, poets, writers, politicians, and magicians looked out a
capacity crowds in the Tabor Opera House on Harrison Avenue and in Eas
Turner Hall on East Third Street. Men and women joined social clubs an
organizations in droves. Over forty-five such "Secret and Benevolen
Societies" were listed in the 1892 *Leadville City Directory,* including th
still-familiar Masons, Knights of Pythias, Odd Fellows, and Elks. Les
familiar were the Improved Order of Red Men, Ancient Order of Foresters
Patriotic Sons of America, Ancient Order of Hiberians, and the Unite
Order of the Golden Cross. Moreover, Leadville always opened its arms t
the Irish, Finns, Germans, Italians, Slovenes, and — except for Chinese –
any immigrants seeking their fortune. To this day one can drive past th
structural remnants of once-thriving Finntown astride East Fifth Street.

The annual Fireman's Ball remained one of the top social events i
Leadville. The glittery affair drew most of Leadville's social elite and thos
aspiring to join their ranks. In the early years "Professor" O. A. Godat directe
the dance, "Professor" A. Fisher directed the "full orchestra," and the Gran

*The date of this unidentified photograph, taken between 1894 and 1898, was
determined by the name of the Leadville photography studio, O'Keefe and
Stockdorf, barely visible on the lower left of the photograph. The young girls'
costumes suggest a Thespian or social group. Fractures in seasoned photographs
like this one convey a greater sense of history.*

A lot of pride was at stake during inter-city fire department competitions. A lot of money changed hands, too. This competition took place on Harrison Avenue. (Courtesy of Bruce and Hillery McCalister)

March commenced at 9 o'clock sharp. Committees responsible for "Reception," "Floor Managers," "Invitation," and "Refreshments," read like the Who's Who list — including the Tabors — of the two-mile-high city.

On some weekends and holidays, especially the Fourth of July, all eyes focused on inter-city firemen tournaments. The competitions centered upon the athletic, with squads competing while unwinding fire hoses from hand-drawn carts, and tossing ladders up against buildings. These were timed competitions — the stuff of high drama — with men, steeds, and equipment from various towns challenging one another. Of course, wagering upon the winner saw numerous pouches of precious mineral dust change hands. Afterward, there was beer, whiskey, cigars, and toasting and boasting all around. A sense of heightened civic security was another byproduct of these firemen's tournaments. Victory parades with the fire laddies decked out in their finest regalia bolstered the conviction that the town had the best fire protection available.

Spot was Leadville's most famous fire dog, attracting almost as much attention as the firemen themselves. For years he skillfully kept town mutts away as the fire horses rushed wagons to the fires. Even the horses were said to have shown a fondness for Spot the fire dog.

But all was not well in mighty Leadville. The price of silver had been steadily declining, while powerful eastern politicians clamored for a return to the gold standard. By the time Leadville saw the gold standard coming, however, it was too late. For years the "silver vs. gold standard" had been debated in newspapers across the United States, especially Leadville's. But it seemed as though the seriousness of the situation fell prey to the psychological mechanisms that prevent humans from thinking about deeply disturbing matters. Simply put, few in Leadville behaved like the price of silver had the slightest chance of falling.

During the early 1890s, Colorado politicians, especially powerful U.S. Senator Henry Teller, did what they could to defeat these powerful eastern "goldbugs," who wanted a gold-backed monetary system. In truth, there was probably nothing Coloradans could have done about it anyway. The general economy of the United States was already in the doldrums, and with the steadily declining price of silver on the world market, several of Britain's mints in India closed on June 26, 1893. More nations throughout the world were turning to gold, rather than silver, to back their currency. The entire West did not have enough clout in Congress to keep the government from buying silver at inflated prices to buoy the bimetallic (silver and gold) monetary system. So, during that fateful July of 1893, when the United States finally repealed the Sherman Silver Purchase Act, the bottom fell out of the price of silver — dropping it to about sixty cents an ounce, less than one-half its value in 1879. Within a week most silver mines in the Leadville Mining District closed, crippling the economy of Leadville.

Fame has not found Henry M. Teller, one of Colorado's first and most influential United States Senators. The well-respected Teller championed silver to the point of fanaticism. (Photograph by M. S. Strain)

The collapse of silver prices in the 1890s strikes most people as nothing more than a bit of uninteresting historical fiscal policy. But, consider the implications. In a matter of days in 1893, a change in the United States government's "uninteresting monetary policy" led to the demise of a silver-mining center, Leadville, which had been the envy of the world for nearly two decades. (Even today few people understand that our specie [coin] and paper currency are no longer backed by either silver or gold. Rather, our money has value only in that people are willing to accept it for goods and services. Should people suddenly decide not to accept our money, because it cannot be exchanged for either silver or gold, it could become worthless overnight.)

Because of the calamitous monetary events, by the summer of 1893 fewer than ten percent of Leadville's work force was employed. Most banks closed. The crime rate and begging soared. A trickle of people leaving the two-mile-high city to seek employment elsewhere increased to a steady stream during the fall of 1893. (Later, westerners, who overwhelmingly favored silver, talked seriously of secession, their zeal fueled by William Jennings Bryan's famous words, "You shall not crucify mankind on a cross of gold.") By 1894, however, when the price of silver climbed slightly, a few downtown mines re-opened, but it was not enough to get Leadville going again. The silver boom days were over. Few would have guessed they would end more quickly than they had began.

Of course, after the panic of 1893, Leadville, like other predominantly silver-mining regions, turned immediately to gold. Rather than seeking new mines, investors focused on further development and refinement of known deposits. Gone were the days of serendipitous discoveries by maverick prospectors. In their place came the new era of methodical and technologically advanced gold mining. A heavily tunneled region between Iowa Gulch and Big Evans Gulch became known as the gold belt. It centered on Breece Hill.

Miners started to turn toward base metals, too. There was plenty of "manganiferous iron that could be used to strengthen steel." A few mines "returned to profitability by selling iron to companies that made railroad car wheels and other steel products. For a while, iron fortified Leadville's weakened economy" (Fogelberg, 2003), but that did not last long either. A recently restored building on Harrison Avenue, the Iron Building, was so named during this less glamorous mining period.

In 1894, two gold mining companies, the Yak Mining, Milling, and Tunnel Company and the Resurrection Gold Mining Company, organized and incorporated. In fact, with little fanfare and virtually no recognition — then or now — these two companies produced impressive amounts of gold. Still, their great nemesis, water, combined with the high cost mining operations, put a damper on their royalties. And unlike Aspen, its flashy rival west of the Continental Divide, Leadville's rock bowels contained, unfortunately, more easily extractable silver than gold.

Leadville's massive ice palace attracted thousands of wide-eyed tourists. An ice colossus welcomed all. (Both W. H. Jackson photographs)

In the winter of 1895-1896, Leadville's will to survive rallied around a truly extraordinary project meant to bolster the city with tourist dollars. The town decided to put on a magnificent Crystal Carnival, part of which was, literally, a colossal "Palace of Ice." People from all over the West flocked to see it. A reporter from the *Salt Lake Democrat* who toured the ice palace gushed, "The effect is of massive architectural beauty, it being of the old Norman school. Its greatest length is 450 feet and its greatest width is 350 feet. Over 8,000 tons of ice were used in its construction. At the front guarding the main entrance is a massive female figure, epresenting the glorification of Leadville" (December 22, 1895). The wed reporter added, "The main chamber of the palace is a skating rink covered by 15,000 square feet of solid ice. On the east is a ballroom and on the west a cafe, all brilliantly lighted by half a hundred arc lights, producing all the rays of the rainbow."

The ice palace was the centerpiece of the Crystal Carnival. But there was more, much more, to welcome the train-loads of excited tourists: toboggan runs, hockey tournaments, tugs of war, drilling contests, and gala balls. Leadville boomed again. Unfortunately this boom lasted only a few months. Atypically warm weather melted the celebrated ice palace in early 1896, along with Leadville's hopes for more tourist dollars. It is to Leadville's credit that the ice palace (and the Crystal Carnival), rather than the silver collapse, is now recalled from this decade. Never mind that it neither attracted enough visitors nor created enough jobs to offset Leadville's economic doldrums for more than a few winter months. At least the Cloud City tried.

Then, just when things started to level off in the summer of 1896, a wave of discontent swept through the overworked and underpaid miners. For years the miners' unions had accepted lower wages and poor benefits (if any) to keep the mines operating. No more, they decreed. On June 21, 1896, 1,600 miners went on strike.

In their classic work, *Geology and Ore Deposits of the Leadville Mining District, Colorado*, Emmons, Irving, and Loughlin (1927) wrote, "The strike that occurred in 1896 closed nearly all the mines for four months and may be regarded as one of the serious strikes in the early history of the western metal industry. Unlike the strike of 1880, it was started by the activities of delegates of the Western Mining Federation of Miners." The trouble arose over decreased wages, after the precipitous decline in silver prices and numerous mine closings.

By July, nearly 2,300 miners were on strike or had been thrown out of work by disgruntled owners. Almost every mine in the Leadville vicinity was affected. Chaos nearly engulfed the

Striking Cloud City miners defiantly pinned ribbons like this one to their chests. (Photograph by M. S. Strain)

city when mine owners tried to bring in miners (scabs) to replace th striking union members.

The "conditions became so threatening that in several of the mines arse nals were installed and armed guards employed" (Emmons et al., 1927) Desperate to get rid of the strike breakers, or "scabs," union member

The Coronado Mine, site of violence and death during Leadville's bitter labor strife.

Soldiers of the Colorado State Militia pose for a photographer at "Camp McIntire." Imagine spending the winter in Leadville in a tent.

decided to blow up the massive fuel oil tank at the Coronado Mine. They started lobbing sticks of dynamite into the mining complex. With the first explosions strikers "began to pour an unrelenting rain of lead into the Coronado buildings and fortifications." Finally, one of the feeder lines ruptured — fuel spewed out of the tank. Within minutes it burst into flames. The fire quickly spread to the superstructure of the mining complex. Leadville Hose Company No. 2 rushed to extinguish the fire. As foreman Jerry O'Keefe, who was partially deaf, seized the nozzle to turn the water full force on the fire, the striking miners shouted at him to stop and go away. He either did not hear, or chose not to respond. No matter, a loud shot rang out from behind, "sending him [O'Keefe] to the earth, bleeding from a mortal wound" (quoted in Blair, 1980).

Shown here are two rare, faded photographs of the strike. Above, a Colorado State Militia soldier keeps watch. Below, although they are difficult to see, soldiers appear to be pointing, or perhaps firing their guns from behind a timber barricade.

From late June until September 20, 1896, there was little mining activity. The labor strife became so bad that it threatened Leadville with anarchy. Finally, Governor Albert W. McIntire ordered the Colorado State Militia to Leadville to quell the violence. Once the militia was called out, "work was resumed on a smaller scale. These conditions continued over a period of nearly nine months, but the transportation of new men [scabs] and the gradual resumption of operations resulted eventually in the defeat of the union, and on March 9, 1897, the strike was declared off" (Emmons et al., 1927). Once again, the miners, even with the backing of their powerful new union, lost.

"The effect of the strike was serious. The production of all classes of ore except high-grade ore fell off enormously." Although the strike terminated in March, the drop in production was all the greater in 1897 because "many of the mines were flooded and had to be pumped out before operations could resume" (Blair, 1980).

For years after the Leadville strike, trouble brewed between mine laborers and owners throughout Colorado. Repeatedly, violence erupted; repeatedly, the Colorado State Militia had to be called out to protect lives and mining property.

By the late 1890s, Leadville's population had fallen to around 12,000, depending on who was doing the counting. Saloons and gambling halls still outnumbered churches ten to one, a ratio indicative, perhaps, of where Leadvillites turned in troubled times. Nevertheless, during the latter half of the decade the Reverends Norlander and Soderstrom faithfully preached to the congregations in The First Evangelical Lutheran Church on the corner of Eighth and Hemlock Streets. (A few years ago a fresh coat of pink paint covered the church, which was transformed into a dance studio.) And

Farther socially than geographically from the infamous State Street, the elegantly appointed Clarendon Hotel Bar (possibly the Midland Bar) on Harrison Avenue catered to the social elite. (Lake County Public Library, Colorado Mountain History Collection)

on December 18, 1899, the laying of the cornerstone of the new St. Joseph's Church merited front-page coverage.

Despite all their troubles, at the close of the 19th century Leadvillites also raised enough money to improve the quality of their children's education. They funded a new high school. Some of the new teachers from the East wrote exhilarating letters home, praising the mountains and excitement that surrounded them. This stately high school structure now serves as part of the National Mining Hall of Fame and Museum, the only national museum in America with a federal charter.

Leadville High School, now part of the National Mining Hall of Fame and Museum, shown during construction.

Only a few businessmen continued to thrive during the post-boom years. One of them was Frank Zaitz. He arrived in Leadville on April 5, 1886. He was seventeen years old. After working in the Arkansas Valley (St. Louis) Smelter for ten years at $2.50 a day, he opened a small saloon at 514 West Chestnut Street. The enterprising Zaitz soon "turned his organizing ability to good use by securing small contracts for unloading coal, coke and other materials at the smelter and the Colorado Midland Railroad" (*Herald Democrat*, December 8, 1994). Next he took a huge financial gamble and opened a comprehensive "shopping center" before such facilities had become a way of life in America. It succeeded because of his hard work and business acumen. Indeed, by the turn of the century this Leadville business stalwart was the largest wholesaler of groceries between Denver and San Francisco. Zaitz never learned to read or write English, but encouraged his fellow Slovenians to do so. Always a generous man, he helped numerous people, including Elizabeth Bonduel Tabor, during his lengthy business career.

As for the Tabor saga, Horace's financial empire had long since collapsed due to poor investments, extended credit, and costly law suits. Still, Elizabeth Bonduel Tabor — contrary to most predictions — stood by her husband, working side by side to help him regain his Midas touch. He never did. Horace Tabor died in 1899. Were it not for his appointment as Postmaster of Denver, Tabor — once the Silver-King and one of the richest men in America — would have died a pauper. His first wife, Augusta, preceded him in death by four years. She died a millionaire. As for Elizabeth Bonduel Tabor, better known as Baby Doe, she would soon move back to Leadville. Thus began one of the most bizarre and intriguing legends in the history of Colorado and the West.

Huge winter storms socked the Cloud City in late 1898 and early 1899, causing intermittent blockages of transportation and work for fifty-seven days. By the end of February in 1899 bone-chilling snowstorms had deposited over fifteen feet of snow on the two-mile-high city. Then it snowed more, a lot more. Cattle starved, horses struggled, people suffered, trains ground to a halt, and deadly snowslides thundered down the steep mountain slopes. It was one of the toughest winters Leadville had ever experienced. In a way it seemed an appropriate ending to a decade that had not been particularly kind to Leadville's fortunes.

Huge snowstorms sealed the decade and the century.

CHAPTER FOUR

Hope and Depression (1900s-1930s)

By the start of the 20th century, Leadville's boom-town atmosphere had long since faded. The Cloud City had metamorphosed into a more typical mountain mining town, struggling to make ends meet. Yet, the publishers of the 1900 *Leadville City Directory* could not resist a little self-promotion, although some might call it self-deception:

> With the issue of the nineteenth annual volume of the Leadville
> City Directory, we are pleased to note that the existing evidences of
> prosperity so plainly visible at the present time are such as to jus-
> tify us in extending our congratulations to the citizens of Leadville
> and all who are interested in the great mining interests over which
> our city is built and surrounded.During the past year a new era in
> our mining industry has been developed which has stimulated con-
> fidence in the permanency and extent of this branch of labor to such
> an extent that it has given employment to a great number of people,

By the turn of the 20th century, Leadville had lost its glow.

and caused activity in building such has not existed in many years. These conditions reach out into all lines of trade and its reviving influence is felt by all classes, causing our city to assume the active appearance of its early years.

In fact, the early 1900s were surprisingly active mining years, and curiously unheralded by historians, with over 4,000 miners employed in the Leadville vicinity. Harking back to the Oro City days, miners once again went in search of gold. This time they did not use pans. Rather, they burrowed and blasted their way deeper into the earth. Their efforts paid off. The first year of the 20th century yielded the highest production of gold in the history of the Leadville Mining District.

The impressive Yak Mill, tunnel, and glistening new power plant brought renewed energy and profit to several mining operations in the region. Between 1901 and 1905 the production of zinc increased substantially as well. The Resurrection No. 1 on Little Ellen Hill, the A.Y. and Minnie on Carbonate Hill, and the Yak Tunnel operation built special mills to help separate the zinc from the ore. Suddenly, things were looking up. Although the Cloud City was no longer the silver capital of the world, it

In the early 1900s a large group of Big Four miners eyed the camera. A few still hold candles although electricity now illuminated most of the subterranean workings.

still had something to
offer people who
chose to make the
two-mile-high city
their home.

On the civic side,
Leadville citizens
behaved more optimistically
than perhaps they had a right
to. Soon after the turn of the
century, the new high school
was completed, and a new
Federal Building and new
Carnegie Public Library were
erected. The two-and-a-half
story Federal Building still
stands on the corner of
Harrison Avenue and Eighth
Street. It housed the post
office until 1973 and now
serves as the city hall and

In 1901 the Colorado Midland Drum Corps played at the "Bal-Masque" in Leadville City Hall.

police station. Fallen police officers are honored on a brass plaque near the
entrance. Nearby, the Carnegie Public Library building still stands on the
corner of East Ninth Street and upper Harrison Avenue. It now houses the
Lake County Civic Center Association's Heritage Museum and Gallery.

In 1905, St. Luke's Hospital acquired Leadville's first ambulance. It was
horse-drawn and equipped with a bell and oil lamps, two on each side. The
"City Record" section in the 1905 *Leadville City Directory* listed Miss M. A.

With the advent of the Environmental Protection Agency, the Yak Tunnel continues to play a role in Leadville history.

Shown here is Leadville's first ambulance. One wonders about the quality of the ride.

McDonald as the "Superintendent" of the hospital. It follows that she must have had the foresight to purchase the ambulance.

During the early 1900s, Leadville had not entirely shorn itself of its long-standing reputation as a wide-open town. Gaming equipment abounded in many of the seventy-three saloons listed in the 1905 *Leadville City Directory.* Nearby these establishments lurked "soiled doves," eager to separate the gamblers from their winnings or wages. A quick inspection of the City Jail Registers during this decade turns up long lists with the names of soiled doves, who were regularly fined five dollars, then released. Such activity obviously provided a constant and sorely needed source of income for the Cloud City's coffers. Not that Leadville could not get help from the current governor, Jesse Fuller MacDonald, a prominent Leadville mine owner who served as Mayor of Leadville before occupying the Capital of Colorado. In the 1980s, MacDonald's fashionably appointed Victorian home at 129 West Eighth Street served as a bed and breakfast.

Then came the Wall Street panic of 1907-1908. Businesses across America suffered. Leadville saw the price of gold struggle to remain steady, while the price of all other metals — save copper — fell. People and businesses began to leave the Cloud City once again, its population falling from approximately 12,000 to 7,000 in less than two years.

America's financial state, including Leadville's, picked up again in the early 1910s. In 1911, when mining had almost ground to a halt, the discovery of more zinc reserves was heralded as Leadville's newest savior. The Wolftone Mine was said to have a body of zinc "so immense that it was measured not in feet, but acres. To celebrate the rebirth of Leadville's mining fortunes, an underground banquet was held deep in the Wolftone Mine on January 25, 1911" (Blair, 1980). The mine's namesake, Wolfe Tone (1763-1798), was the father of Irish republicanism.

Locally, mining engineers also attacked their major mining nemesis: water. By 1912, beneath the Yak Mill, workers had completed a "drainage, prospecting and tramway tunnel from southwest slope of Iron hill in California gulch, just above the power station, to Diamond mine in Evans gulch, about four and one-half miles" (Gilfillan and Gilfillan, 1964). With lower water levels, several of the workings intersected by this water-drainage tunnel resumed successful mining operations.

Several downtown mines that had been closed during the 1907-1908 panic lay dormant for years. They quickly filled with water. In 1914 local engineers pumped out the water, mining resumed, and Leadville's overall production of gold and several base metals once again increased.

Leadvillites had not lost their thirst for alcohol. In 1915, the Cloud City boasted two breweries, three liquor dealers, and fifty-five saloons. In 1916, when Colorado "went dry," none of the exact names of these establishments, not one, appeared on the pages of the *Leadville City Directory*. Yet it seems fair to speculate that the city's thirst for alcohol had not diminished since many of these establishments remained in business, albeit under different

Wolftone employees and their guests are shown in this poor quality photograph during their underground banquet. (Lake County Public Library, Colorado Mountain History Collection)

A portion of a 1913 panorama by photographer B. C. Gray captured Leadville in transition. To the left the Vendome Stage, that shuttled passengers to and from the train depot, was — fittingly — obscured by the immensely popular automobile. Riders on each side of the photograph straddled their new-fangled, and equally popular motorcycles. A motorized fire engine occupied the middle.

names. True to its reputation, Leadville soon became known throughout the state as a good place to buy illegal booze. Gambling, now also illegal, thrived as well. Even righteous crusaders like District Attorney Barney L. Whatley, who burned confiscated gaming devices at the city dump, could not entirely suppress Leadville's underground gaming or drinking.

On April 6, 1917, the United States declared war on Germany and its allies. During the next two years, with brass bands blaring, thousands upon thousands of young men, including many from Leadville, innocently marched off to save the world. Brutal trench warfare quickly quelled their enthusiasm, if they survived. Written on the chalk board in the following photograph was:

> *Call No. 1807. Enlistment for Colorado. Agricultural College Fort Collins. Men who are physically qualified for general military service and have a Grammar School Education or at least four years of Schooling in the following branches: Auto Mechanics, General Mechanics, Concrete Workers, Horse Shoers, Radio Operators. Enlistments Close Aug-6-1918.*

In 1918 and 1919 more than 20,000,000 people world-wide died as the result of one of the worst flu epidemics, and human catastrophes, on record.

As it swept through the Cloud City, it sent several hundred of its citizens to their graves. The death toll averaged ten a day for several months. Closing the schools and banning indoor gatherings did little to stop the spread of the deadly virus. Because of the heating facilities in the Clarendon Hotel, it was leased for use as a hospital. Many women (see page 54) bravely volunteered to help the sick and dying in the once-elegant Clarendon. "Not all of them [women volunteers] are from select circles" (Griswold and Griswold, 1971), meaning prostitutes helped too. "The mortuaries were hard pressed to supply coffins and keep up with the funerals" (Manly, 1980).

As if this deadly epidemic was not enough, another miners' strike and the end of the war in 1919 closed most of Leadville's mines again, and again water filled the shafts and tunnels. Then the price of zinc dropped.

But hope springs eternal, especially in mining towns. At the end of this decade Leadvillites turned their eyes toward yet another metallic savior: molybdenum, a grayish element used to harden alloy steels and soften tungsten alloy. Although it had been discovered by gold miners in Climax in 1900 on Mt. Bartlett (northeast of town near Fremont Pass), no steel companies seemed interested in it. There was literally a mountain of it. Max Schott organized the Climax Molybdenum Company in 1917, but

Ribbons emblazoned with "NATIONAL ARMY, LAKE COUNTY, COLORADO" adorned their lapels. Recruits, dressed in their Sunday best, held bags stuffed with recruitment materials. Several of them, including the one with the short pants and white shoes in the front row, looked apprehensive, and well they should have.

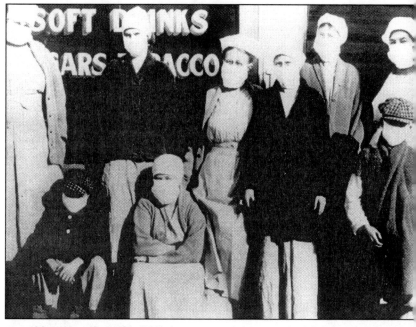

Breathing through masks did little to prevent the spread of the deadly influenza that took millions of lives throughout the world in 1918 and again in 1919. (Lake County Public Library, Colorado Mountain History Collection)

the ore simply piled up because there was so little demand for it. In 1918 the mine shut down. No one could have guessed that the Climax Molybdenum Mine would someday out produce the entire Leadville Mining District.

During the late 1920s, the Cloud City continued to languish while it citizens clung to dreams of renewed prosperity. Surely not a single fortune seeker who experienced the excitement and chaos of the 1870s and 1880s could have imagined that Leadville would come to this. There were eerily abandoned side streets, and often not a soul to see on Harrison Avenue, once called "the main street of American mining." Harsh winter storms steadily battered the few remaining cribs and saloons on the once famous State Street. Many did not mourn State Street's demise. Even today one can stroll down the infamous State Street (present-day West Second Street). On dark winter nights, when frigid winds howl through the dilapidated buildings that remain, some tourists claim to have heard the plaintive voices of the soiled doves.

In 1922, some influential citizens in Leadville sponsored the Canterbury Tunnel, meant to drain water from the extensive workings on Carbonate Hill. Insufficient funds doomed the project from the beginning. And 1921

Few of the revelers on early State Street could have imagined this sorry sight.
(Lake County Public Library, Colorado Mountain History Collection)

By the 1930s, men loading silver bullion into the Colorado Midland's rolling
stock was a scene from the past.

had already been described as Leadville's worst year ever. The Colorado Midland Railway shut down its line in 1923. In 1926, a Denver & Rio Grande Western engine and six cars plunged into the river a few miles south of Leadville, injuring over fifty people and killing twenty-nine. It was the worst wreck in Arkansas Valley history. On top of all this came the 1929 crash of Wall Street, and the ensuing economic depression. Some feared that their two-mile-high city might soon become a ghost town, a phenomenon not unheard of in high-country Colorado.

By the early 1930s, Leadville's population — barely 4,000 souls and shrinking fast — did not even have a bank to serve them. Times were tough, real tough. People carrying sacks could be seen collecting chunks of coal along railroad tracks. Everyone scrimped, saved, and reused everything they could. Brewing moonshine liquor reached new heights. Those fortunate few who had jobs or access to economic resources found dignified ways to help relatives, friends, and often as not, strangers. As for mining, it was basically finished. Some miners attempted to earn a living by reworking old tailings or mine dumps. A few skeleton crews, who never experienced the boom times, kept mines like the Resurrection (below), R.A.M, and Greenback open. They had to work hard to scratch out a meager living. Parenthetically, the R.A.M. was more renown for its name than its ore. Prospectors who discovered the R.A.M. swore that its location on a steep hillside forced them to slide on their britches down to the road

Few mines remained open during the 1930s. Those that did employed few miners.

Leadville still loved its football, too, especially when the team won. (The
Prospector, 1929 Leadville High School Annual)

in Stray Horse Gulch. The recorder, however, would not allow the name
Ragged Ass Mine to be entered officially into the records. So R.A.M. it was.

On a happier note for many of the townspeople, in 1932, with the
repeal of the Prohibition Act, a parade was held for "Old Man Prohibition."
A horse-drawn hearse, once used to transport the bodies of women and
children to the Leadville cemetery, carried a casket with "Old Man
Prohibition" himself, who was properly buried by a preacher and mourners
near the present Fifth Street ball diamond — baseball being one of
Leadville's favorite pastimes, along with drinking.

In 1934, Congress adopted the Gold Reserve Act, meaning that the government abandoned the gold standard just as it had abandoned the silver
standard forty years earlier. Simultaneously, the United States Mint
stopped minting gold coins and individuals could no longer hold gold
except for rare coins. That same year Congress passed the Silver Purchase
Act, "which established the nationalization of domestic silver holdings
until the price reached a predetermined level" (Bunyak, 2003). Although
these monetary moves sound ominous, unlike forty years earlier, when the
repeal of the Sherman Silver Purchase Act crippled Leadville, the 1934
Gold Reserve Act and the Silver Purchase Act did not affect the price of
silver substantially. It did cause a "rise in gold prices from $20.67 to $35.00
per ounce, [and] the mining regions of the West enjoyed a moderate boom
period" (Bunyak, 2003).

More Leadville eyes, however, were starting to look toward Climax. By
now Climax had completed its new half-mile Wills tunnel (named for the
early automobile) that connected the mill directly to the ore reserves. This
allowed for a substantial increase in ore production at reduced costs.

Combined with an increasing demand for molybdenum, a total of 280 men worked in the mill, tunnel, and mine in general.

Ever a sporting town, Leadville continued to support its teams despite the hard economic times. Basketball remained especially popular in the two-mile-high city throughout the long, cold winters. During summer, motorcycle racers vied for victory as they roared around an elliptical track. In the track's infield, the crack of baseball bats could be heard coming from the baseball diamond. Leadville High School overlooked the track and baseball field from the north side of West Ninth Street.

Throughout the 1930s, in obvious desperation, Leadville continued to place its hope for economic salvation in metallic saviors. "Gold Ore Deposits Of District Await Coming of Capital: Promising Areas Long Neglected Have Boundless Possibilities — Careful Study of Geological Conditions Should Be Made," read the typical headline in the *Herald Democrat* in 1932. "Roosevelt May Boost Silver Price to $1.19," pined the *Carbonate Chronicle* in 1933, claiming that such a price would result "in the biggest boom the West has seen in years." Also on the front pages were melancholy reminders of H.A.W. Tabor: "New Biography of Tabor Makes Fascinating Reading," and "Mining Associate of Tabor is Dead." It seemed as though Leadville's citizens could not let go of the former boom-town glory. Who could blame them?

But they did let go — psychologically at least — of Horace Tabor's second wife. Indeed, a casual reader of Leadville newspapers would not have known that Mrs. Elizabeth Bonduel Tabor had lived in Leadville since the early 1900s. Yet every local knew she did. It is just that her presence did not bring back positive thoughts about the glory days. Rather, her haunting figure and pathetic circumstance, especially during the 1920s and early 1930s, made most people who encountered her ponder the cruel capriciousness of the fates.

To search for *the* historic Elizabeth Bonduel "Baby Doe" Tabor, at least after 1900, is hopeless. Too many people have told too many stories, including well-known writers. Caroline Bancroft gets credit for the biggest whopper. It turns out, according to a recent *Colorado Heritage* magazine article (Riley, 2002), that Horace's dying command to Baby Doe, "Hang on to the Matchless," was never uttered. The five most famous words in Colorado history were fabrications? Apparently so. "Well," Bancroft responded to a colleague's comment on the beauty of the famous words, "I made them up."

Details of the second Mrs. Tabor's life are also confusing and contradictory. Traditional historical wisdom holds that Elizabeth Bonduel Tabor moved into the small cabin, better described as a shack, at the Matchless Mine on the outskirts of Leadville between 1899 and 1903.

Baby Doe

TABOR

1884

and

1934

--- * ---

Matchless
Mine,

Leadville,
Colo.

Myth and reality mix in the incredible life-story of Elizabeth Bonduel "Baby Doe" Tabor. Here she walks out the door of her cabin. (Courtesy of Barb Bost)

Yet, all one has to do is look in the local *Leadville City Directories* to find the first reference to her is in 1905: "Tabor H. A. W., Mrs. rms. 303 Harrison av." Further research shows this address to be the Clarendon Hotel. Then, for the next three years, the entry is the same: "Tabor H. A. W. Mrs., r. [residence] Matchless Mine, head E. 12th." In 1909 she disappears from the listings, but not the shack. As for the shack, it was a single room (with a small wood-shed), thinned-walled, poorly constructed wooden affair with a detached outhouse. Spending even one of Leadville's brutal, long winters in such a place was neither for the meek nor weak. Now imagine what it took to spend *thirty years* within its Spartan confines. Then consider the contrast to Elizabeth's years of living in absolute luxury, the pampered wife of one of the richest men in the West.

Some say Baby Doe defended her cabin with a shotgun; others say she welcomed visitors. Some say she was crazy as a loon; others say she was as sane as could be. Some say she had no close friends; others say George M. Schmidt, a "dwarfed and eccentric sour dough miner" (*Leadville Boom Days*, 1977), lived close to her and watched out for her until he died in 1930. Some say she readily accepted food placed by her door; others say she tossed it away. And some say she knew very well that her youngest child, Silver Dollar, died an alcohol-and-drug-addicted prostitute under mysterious circumstances in Chicago in 1925 at the age of thirty-six. Others say Elizabeth Tabor absolutely believed that Silver Dollar was in a

During better times, Silver Dollar Tabor greeted President Theodore Roosevelt on August 29, 1910. (Courtesy of Barb Bost)

convent, a ruse Silver Dollar tried to maintain with her deeply concerned and psychologically troubled mother.

There can be no doubt, however, that Elizabeth Tabor lived at the Matchless Mine for the better part of thirty years. Nor can there be any doubt that the books and movie (the opera came later) about her life attracted attention throughout the United States while she was still living in a shack beside the Matchless Mine. "Elizabeth had been outraged in 1932 by the publication of David Karsner's sensationalized book about her *Silver Dollar*, which was followed by a Hollywood film that drew huge crowds to its Denver premiere. She wrote to friends, "I am breaking my heart of that Book and that Picture Show" (Temple, 2001). Nor is there any doubt that her first child, Lily, called the "Most beautiful child in the world," moved back to the Midwest. From then on, according to some historians, Lily claimed to be Baby Doe's cousin, not daughter. Lastly, there can be no doubt that Elizabeth Tabor slowly but surely fell victim to her own psychological demons.

Held within the archives of the Colorado Historical Society are thousands, perhaps as many as 50,000, pieces of paper in all sizes, shapes, and forms in a series of archival storage files. Most of the paper contains the handwriting of Elizabeth Tabor. She wrote and scribbled the vast majority of these notes and letters during her decades-long vigil at the Matchless Mine, even though Horace had not told her to hang on to it. A recent article in *Colorado Heritage* by Judy Nolte Temple carries the title, "The Demons of Elizabeth Tabor, Mining 'Dreams and Visions' from the Matchless." Temple writes, "Up in that cabin she religiously, obsessively wrote thousands of accounts — [of] her Dreams and Visions." For the first

*Sun Nov 12-1922 I dreamed of being in a large
open place light & bright & like Machenry
in the place or something of its kind, my Mother
was with us very strong & fine she had a grand
new rich dress with an old fashoned full
round skirt like they used to wear over
big hoops & Mothers looked as if she had
on hoops for the big dress skirt looks as if
it was stretched tight over hoops & it was
of bright collars of threads running round
is like corordroy good, but her dress was of
rich goods not `` `` she was happy & grand
& walking around & Sister Lilly* [here
Elizabeth spells her eldest daughter's
name as "Lilly."] *was there
with us also more of our family & O
such a beautiful baby about 2 or 3 years
old She was fat & plump with pink cheeks
& lovely complexion & wonderful eyes so
big round & so blue with golden yellow
hair & she was dressed rich with hood
on & her Eyes sparkled & so bright & they
looked at me & she watched me all the time
& she kept close to me she was a gorgous
baby & her beautiful face was large & she
was so happy, I said "O Lilly what a
beautiful Baby you have she is O so
lovely so grand," I thought we were all
there together because it was all about
the Matchless Mine I thought & me all had
something to do about Matchless. &
think the Baby means `` Mine is —
going to be worked at once_ That
God is now ready to stop all
the devils thieves and enemies
God our—Divine Jesus Christ our
Savior Knows what is best for
us all, and especially for those who
worship Him does he cut the time
short & help them always. Bless
Be God forever*

**Transcription of a hand-written note on a piece of
Vendome Hotel stationery. (Courtesy of the Collection
of George R. Cassidy)**

Papers lay scattered across the floor of Elizabeth Tabor's cabin shortly after her death. (Courtesy of Barb Bost)

Ramblings of a tormented and confused mind. Here Elizabeth Tabor wrote on a Hostess wrapper. (Courtesy of the Collection of George R. Cassidy)

time, Temple tries to make some psychological sense out of the mass of scribblings bequeathed to us by the tormented Tabor. Temple's scholarly attempt is worth reading, as is John Burke's, *The Legend of Baby Doe, The Life and Times of the Silver Queen of the West.*

Included here (pages 61 and 62) are two of Baby Doe's hand-written notes from the late 1920s. They are rare and revealing. They offer a personal, poignant glimpse into the tormented psychological world of Elizabeth Tabor during her self-imposed isolation of so many years.

Perhaps, however, it wasn't so lonely or tormented, if on occasion, she had such beautiful sights to see.

On March 7, 1935, Elizabeth Bonduel Tabor's legendary life ended. Her body was found frozen in her shack, bundled in rags with her feet wrapped in newspapers. To this day, hundreds of people make the pilgrimage to her shack at the Matchless. There they find the legend, not the lady.

As for the economic fortunes of Leadville in 1935, they were dismal. In a doubly cruel economic and symbolic blow, the small, but still important Colorado & Southern Railroad abandoned its 150 miles of track to Leadville in 1935, then soon thereafter the once-dominant Denver & Rio Grande quit Leadville as well. The Denver & Rio Grande Western passenger train chugged through the Cloud City for the last time on November 16, 1939. Only one passenger peered out at the once mighty boom town.

Something had to be done to diversify Leadville's economy. It was finally getting through to the dwindling populace that mining could no longer sustain them. So local merchants turned to something new, something not tried systematically since the Crystal Carnival of the late 19th century: tourism. Why not take advantage of the revolution in independent transportation? Almost everyone owned a car, and Leadville was "on several of the best highways from Denver, Colorado Springs, Pueblo and Cañon City, on the east and south, to Glenwood Springs, Grand Junction and northwestern Colorado." Shiny silver brochures touted Leadville as "the heart of Vacation Land — where dreams of a glorious summer outing come true" in "the finest summer climate in the world in the midst of majestic mountains under Colorado's turquoise sky." The boosterism continued, "Beautiful and convenient campsites in every gulch and valley in our pine-clad hills, along tumbling trout streams, or by shores of deep-hued lakes await you." For the more adventuresome, tourists could drive their autos through the two-mile "Carlton Tunnel" (an old Colorado Midland Railway tunnel) under the Continental Divide on the way to Glenwood Springs, Basalt, or Aspen. But the tourists did not come, at least not in the numbers Leadvillites had hoped for.

It must have been a thrill to drive through this abandoned two-mile-long Colorado Midland Tunnel.

CHAPTER FIVE

Camp Hale, Climax, and Community (1940s-1960s)

Like other towns in America, Leadville saw changes brought about by World War II. Rationing of gas, certain foods, tires, and other materials deemed crucial for the war served as daily reminders, along with the newspaper headlines, of the deadly seriousness of the war. Not that Leadville citizens needed to be reminded as they watched, once again, a number of their young men march off to war in Europe and the Pacific as well. The war also brought about a momentary revival of mining in the early 1940s due to artificially inflated prices. Mining throughout the United States perked up again. In Lake County, the Resurrection properties in Big Evans Gulch profited the most. The biggest change in Leadville, however, resulted from a decision by the United States Army to construct a large training camp for their new "Mountain Troops" just over Tennessee Pass to the north of town. The Mountain Troops, forerunners of the now famous 10th Mountain Division, had been created in November 1941.

Preliminary construction of the camp began on April 10, 1942, near an old Denver & Rio Grande Railway stop named Pando, on a broad valley

Camp Hale spread out across the entire Eagle Valley floor. (Lake County Public Library, Colorado Mountain History Collection)

Soldiers practice firing mortars during winter. One wonders if such sessions triggered avalanches. (Lake County Public Library, Colorado Mountain History Collection)

floor at an elevation of 9,500 feet. Within a year, a small city, named Camp Hale after Colorado's own Brigadier General Irving Hale, blossomed along the entire valley floor. It took over 11,000 workers and railroad carload after railroad carload of machinery and equipment to complete the job. Over 200,000 cubic yards of dirt and rock were dumped onto the Eagle Valley floor. Long streets lined with rows of barracks quickly crisscrossed the broad valley. The Eagle River was diverted into a ditch paralleling the streets that adjoined it.

The modern military camp bustled with hundreds of hand-picked young men, "many of them ski experts, mountain climbers, trappers, guides, sportsmen, and even prospectors" (Cassidy, M., 1983). Their equipment included specially designed clothing, skis, snowshoes, motorized winter vehicles, pack animals, and even "midget mountain stoves." The whole point of this experimental camp (for nothing like it had ever been done before) was to train these troops to live and fight under the most rigorous winter conditions in the most forbidding mountain terrain.

By 1943, "the experimental stage of training came to an end with the activation of the 10th Mountain Division under the command of Brigadier General Lloyd Jones" (Cassidy, M., 1983). For almost a year, the 10th

Mountain Division underwent regular infantry combat training combined with special training for combat in high altitudes and temperatures well below zero degrees Fahrenheit. "Men who had never seen skis put them on . . . then glided down slight slopes, and later to use trails fanning out along the summit of the longest Constam ski lift in the world, located on Cooper Hill" (Cassidy, M., 1983). Ironically, these "ski troopers," as they came to be called, seldom saw action on skis. Rather, they used their rock-climbing

skills the most, where they "were crucial in a predawn raid of River Ridge, a pivotal battle now commemorated by a ski run at Vail" (*Denver Post*, June 1, 2003).

Of course, many Leadville businesses profited from the construction of Camp Hale and the patronage of its soldiers and workers. Local citizens frequently planned special U.S.O. activities to entertain the troops and show their appreciation for their training efforts. Bars, restaurants, and theaters in town were often packed to overflowing by soldiers from Camp Hale. Military authorities

During war the soldiers' rock-climbing skills proved to be as important, if not more, than their skiing skills. (Lake County Public Library, Colorado Mountain History Collection)

Camp Hale even had its own newspaper, the appropriately named Ski-Zette.

however, soon designated the once-infamous State Street, which seemed to experience a bit of a revival, as officially "off limits" to all military personnel. (Rumors continue to circulate that the world's oldest profession remained active on State Street well into the 1960s.)

In 1985, the 10th Mountain Division veterans' organization still had 3,000 members, the largest military organization for a deactivated unit in the history of the Army. Clearly, these men had formed a special bond. Well they should have, for during 144 days of combat on the German front in the Italian Alps, they lost 992 of their comrades, with 4,154 wounded. After the war, a few men of the 10th Mountain Division returned to pioneer some of the better known ski areas in the world, Aspen and Vail among them.

Even before World War II officially ended, according to some accounts, German prisoners of war tore down the 245 barracks and most of the other buildings. In 1966 the Forest Service took control of the final portion of the 247,000 acre military reservation. Ceremonies commemorating the bravery of the 10th Mountain Division are still held each Memorial Day atop Tennessee Pass where the names of the men are memorialized on fitting monuments.

In June 1942 tragedy struck the Leadville community. It was a sight no Leadvillite, or Coloradan, wanted to see: the venerable Lake County Courthouse was consumed by flames. Built on the west side of Harrison

The Lake County Courthouse, seen in the background of this photograph from the early 1940s, soon burned. Here the old Leadville Hose Company's (No. 2) classic four-wheeled carriage helps celebrate the Fourth of July. (Lake County Public Library, Colorado Mountain History Collection)

The hose wheel and lamps of Leadville's Hose Company (No. 2) carriage can be seen in the foreground of this tragic image of the Lake County Courthouse burning. (Lake County Public Library, Colorado Mountain History Collection)

Avenue during 1879, the imposing courthouse had stood as a symbol of community pride for over sixty years. It was designed by prominent Leadville architect George King. In 1885, a popular Colorado tourist guide (Crofutt, 1885) proclaimed that the courthouse "would do credit to many cities 10 times the population." The upper floor received the most damage. Years later the refurbished first floor proved too crowded, so the entire building was razed. Since 1955, a new courthouse on the same location physically, although not aesthetically, has filled the void.

From its inception,

Leadville never ducked a parade or special community event. In 1940 local citizens held the first annual Tabor Days. Three days of activities featured a Sunday of "Soft Ball, Fly Casting, Horse Shoe Pitching, First Aid Contest, and State Championship Machine Rock Drilling" in between "Children's Day" and a "Parade Day" complete with five-foot long banners sporting a likeness of "H.A.W. TABOR." As the program proclaimed, "You Can't Beat Fun the Leadville Way." Leadville's "2nd Annual Tabor Days"

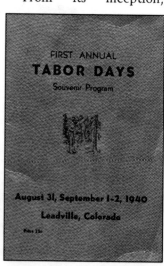

Shown here is an original program of the First Annual Tabor Days. (Courtesy of Bruce and Hillery McCalister)

featured dancing every night with "Henry King — Direct from Hollywood — and His Orchestra with a Host of Stars, All in Person."

In late 1943 Paramount Pictures crews came to Leadville as well. A group of twenty-one cameramen took background shots for "I Love a Soldier," starring Paulette Goddard and Sonny Tufts. Camp Hale ski troopers, dressed in their all-while uniforms, also appeared in the motion picture. A few other movie crews shot scenes in Leadville and the picturesque Arkansas Valley, but the Cloud City could not sustain its Hollywood image for long.

If the truth be known, for several decades Leadville had been known as a deteriorating, insignificant mining town. As soon as the war ended the prices of most metals fell, sending most of the United States's mining industry, including Leadville, into yet another tailspin. In the 1950s Leadville citizens looked around at their beloved, drab town and decided that it was time for a substantial facelift —and more. The Cloud City began by building a new sewer system and treatment plant. Then it constructed new schools, a new courthouse, a new lodge for the Elks, a

Mrs. Florence Hollister purchased the Elks Opera House in 1954. She not only saved it from demolition, she restored its original name: The Tabor Opera House.

small though modern medical center, a new hospital, a modern bank, and even a new $175,000 Labor Center. The Lake County Recreational Board was also formed. So too, construction began on several new homes on the west side of town. In short, the 7,000 or so denizens of Leadville had reason to take pride in their civic accomplishments, even though plenty of deserted, dilapidated homes and buildings remained in the town and the surrounding mining areas.

Perhaps the most historic edifice, thanks to the pluck and perseverance of one family, was, and still is, used for good purpose. In 1954, members of the Elks Lodge voted unanimously to sell the historic Tabor Opera House, which had been their headquarters under the name of "Elk's Opera House" since 1900, to Mrs. Florence Hollister for $20,000. She alone probably saved it from demolition. Her daughter, Mrs. Evelyn Livingston Furman, later refurbished portions of the historic building, and wrote books about it and the Tabors. Like her mother before her (often with the help of her close friend Theresa O'Brien), Evelyn personally guided stimulating tours for delighted tourists. Now her daughter and son-in-law carry on the admirable family tradition.

Inside the Tabor Opera House, a hand-painted scene of the Royal Gorge graced the main curtain, with eight drop-curtains behind, some of which are used in current productions. A thirty-five by fifty-five foot stage equipped with trap doors could handle large operas, animal shows, magic shows, bands, and boxing matches. A large dressing room for the chorus, several small ones for the players, and a special one for the star were all situated under the stage. A massive coal furnace provided ample heat for the house on even the coldest winter nights. Seventy-two gas jets illuminated, when necessary, the entire house. Like everything else used in the building, the original cast iron, red plush opera chairs were the best money could buy. Most of the 880 chairs installed in 1879 remain.

This exquisite opera house was the centerpiece of Leadville in the late 1870s, and it remains the historically priceless centerpiece of downtown Leadville. Although the "Ballad of Baby Doe" made its debut at the Central City Opera House in 1956, with a cast of several Metropolitan Opera singers, it has since been performed before enthralled crowds in the place and city where its heart is: at the Tabor Opera House in Leadville. Tourists from throughout Colorado and the United States still eagerly sign the old registration book before taking tours of this grand old structure. Unfortunately, like in most small towns across America during this era, few historic buildings of this magnificent caliber received such respect.

Early in the 1950s, when Leadville started to put on its bright new face, it did so, some complained, with a vengeance. It was all in with the new, out with the old. Leadville historian, Edward Blair, wrote about Leadville's new direction, "So extensive and so complete was the transformation that *Look Magazine*, in its February 17, 1959, issue, named Leadville one of its All America City award recipients . . . . For the first time in Leadville's history she took no pride in her uniqueness. For the first time in her history she wanted to be Anytown, U.S.A." (Blair, 1980). Blair shied away from witching Leadville's emphasis to skiing, mountain recreation, and "history as a saleable commodity," though he strongly favored historical preservation. Of the All America City designation in the late 1950s, Blair wrote, "Leadville was still a mining town, a one-industry town, and open to the vicissitudes of the mining industry." As for the boom-bust cycles of the mining industry, Blair would prove to be right.

Leadville received a poignant reminder of its mining legacy in 1958 when a nearly two-month long strike shut down the Climax Molybdenum mining complex completely. It was settled on October 10, 1958. Another longer-lasting, bitter strike at Climax with enduring negative feelings occurred between July 1962 and January 1963.

In 1960, with Leadville's population hovering around 4,000, the county purchased the old Liberty Bell Theatre, tore it down, and replaced it with grass. In 1879, the community lovingly constructed its first hospital, St. Vincent's. In the early 1960s the community tore old St. Vincent's down. An historic bank, Hunter and Trimble's, found itself dismantled and shipped to Aspen. The historic and irreplaceable back-bar in the Pioneer Saloon went out the door — not without notice and some regret — to Fat City, California. Then fire claimed "several lives and the Union Block, built in 1887 by Tabor and the Guggenheims, the DeMain[e]ville Block, constructed about the same time, and the historic home of William H. James, located immediately south of the Healy House" (Blair, 1980). Many historic homes were dismantled or destroyed.

Climax Molybdenum Mine near Fremont Pass did not find itself immune to the boom-bust cycles of the mining industry.

Also in 1960, Climax, which still employed over 2,000 workers, decided to, literally, move their company town to Leadville. "They planned to move the whole community into a subdivision they had started months before in an area north and west of Leadville's city limits" (Blair, 1980), soon named West Park. In fact, they held a contest to name the new subdivision. The reward: a free home.

Dick Beauford owned the company that moved the town of Climax to Leadville. With 45 workers, Beauford's company took three years to move 370 houses, apartments, and garages to the West Park area. "Dick was driving the truck that pulled the only house that was dropped during the entire operation. And that house belonged to Dr. Elzi, who was the head of our Clinic [Climax's] for many years. The insurance company said there was $4,500 damage, but the baby grand piano that was inside the house didn't even receive a scratch" (*Hi Grade*, September 9, 1979). Although the houses made the twelve-mile trip to Leadville fairly easily, it took almost nine hours to haul each of the three-story apartment buildings. Once set up, house prices in West Park ranged between $5,000 and $10,000.

As for mining in the 1960s, the American Smelting and Refining Company finally shut down its Leadville operation, as did the Arkansas Valley Smelter, the longest continuing business in the Leadville Mining District. There was simply not enough mining activity to support them. Climax hired many of the miners who were laid off. Railroad buffs mourned the sound of the last steam engine chugging into town. Even the sounds of Arkansas Valley were changing.

The Climax molybdenum mining complex now constituted the heart and soul of the region's mining activities. In 1962, the Climax Molybdenum

Most of these Climax Molybdenum Company houses ended up twelve miles away in West Park, Leadville.

Company mined over 36,000 tons of ore per day. According to the Colorado Bureau of Mines, the Climax Company grossed over $46,695,020 (even with the strike), or forty percent of Colorado's metallic minerals production. Moreover, the decision to uproot their company town was based on their desire to begin open-pit mining where the town once stood.

The opening of the Joint Venture's Irene shaft and the sinking of the Black Cloud shaft constituted the only other notable mining activity of the decade in the 1960s. In February 1970, the Black Cloud shaft, located about five miles south of Leadville in the Iowa Gulch District at 11,087 feet elevation, "bottomed at 1,655 feet with stations having been cut at the 550, 900, 1250, and 1500 feet levels. Stations were also cut for a pump room and an underground crusher" (*Leadville Boom Days*, 1984).

Steve Voynick (1996), in his superlative book, *Climax: The History of Colorado's Climax Molybdenum Mine*, documented the importance of this mining company to the economic and cultural well-being of Leadville and Lake County. During the 1960s and throughout most of the 1970s Climax provided up to 3,000 workers with respectable wages. This translated into Lake County having the highest per capita income, $21,000, in the state. In the early 1960s Climax accounted for 96 percent of the bond issue for establishing Colorado Mountain College in Leadville. They also paid the majority (86 percent one year) of Lake County's property taxes. Millions of these dollars profited the school district. As if that was not enough, Climax granted college scholarships topping $1,000,000. Their generosity also extended to numerous cultural and social activities in the community. Before long, it became hard to imagine Leadville or Lake County without Climax's huge presence and support.

Although the Tabor Days were no more, the cities of Fairplay and Leadville, located on opposite sides of the Continental Divide, had cooperatively held the "World's Championship Pack Burro Race, Running Fairplay to Leadville" for almost two decades. This unusual event was run over Mosquito Pass between the two old mining towns. The course, formerly an old stagecoach trail and wagon trail, was twenty-three miles in length, reaching an elevation of 13,182 feet at the highest point. "Each burro is equipped with a regulation pack saddle, and twenty-five pounds of weight. Each contestant is required to walk, run or even carry his burro, but is not allowed to ride at any time. Persuasive implements are allowed to further increase the progress of the burro" (*Seventeenth Annual Pack Burro Race* booklet).

In 1969, long-standing disagreements over some specifics of the race resulted in Leadville and Fairplay each staging their own. Since then Leadville contestants have urged their burros to the top of Mosquito Pass, then raced back down into town. The Burro Race now caps off the Cloud

Note that in 1961 (left) the Thirteenth Annual World's Championship Pack Burro Race still took place between Fairplay and Leadville. By 1970 (right) Leadville and Fairplay held their own races. (Both courtesy of Barb Bost)

City's Boom Day festivities held to commemorate and celebrate Leadville's founding. There are numerous mining-related activities, contests, and a full schedule of social events.

As for what was to come before the close of the 20th century, Leadvillites, battered by boom-bust cycles, hesitated to speculate. Worse, the population continued to decline slowly. Some moved out of the state, some moved to Denver — the monstrous metropolis lurking only a hundred miles away and 5,000 feet lower — and others, ever optimistic, remained in their two-mile-high city. At least there would always be the mighty Climax Molybdenum Company.

CHAPTER SIX

Past Meets Present (1970s-2000s)

In 1916 Charlyle Channing Davis, early Leadville pioneer and publisher, wrote, "There has been but one Leadville. Never will there be another" (*Olden Times in Colorado*). People unfamiliar with the Cloud City might think that the once great mining boom town has disappeared. It has not. Rather, the past has met the present in Leadville. During the last few decades the community has made some wise decisions, both big and small, that bode well for its future. That is not to say that Leadville is problem free, or does not face daunting challenges. It does. But what town doesn't? And Leadville has the advantage of working with an unparalleled history in an exquisite mountain setting.

In the early 1970s, Leadville began to take more notice of its history. Today it is not news when cities throughout America scramble to learn more about their past as well as preserve their historic structures and neighborhoods that have managed to dodge the bulldozer. Historical awareness and preservation *was* new in the 1970s. Early on came the Lake County Civic Center Association [LCCCA]. Its first president, Edward Blair, wrote (1981):

> The origins of the LCCCA predate its organization by almost two years. It began innocently enough. I was teaching in the junior high school at the time and was suffering from my first cold of the season. I stopped by the Clinic for a cure and I met John Pitts coming out. He greeted me, "Blair, when are you going to do something about the loss of all this Leadville material?"
> "Why me, John? Why don't you do something?"
> "No, no!" he replied, shaking his open hand at me. "You're the one that has to do it."
> "Will you help?"
> "Yes."

The next weekend there was a meeting at the Healy House Museum. By the end of 1969 the Colorado Mountain Historical Association came to life. (A few years later, after a number of political machinations, the fledgling society took the cumbersome name, Lake County Civic Center Association [LCCCA].) Soon John Pitts coordinated the first two Leadville History courses. "It was for a long time the largest single class taught at Colorado Mountain College, with over seventy paid registrants. The second class was held at the cafeteria at Pitts Elementary School, again with almost seventy people enrolled" (Blair, 1981).

In 1973 came the Association's first historical periodical, *Mountain Diggings*. It focused exclusively on Leadville and Lake County history. "That fall the essay contest was created, with the Don and Jean Griswold Award for the best adult entry and the Poppy Smith Award for the best student entry" (Blair, 1981). *Mountain Diggings* continued to be published for sixteen years with a steady readership among Leadville citizens concerned about the

disposition of the Cloud City's heritage as well as the Cloud City's future. Meanwhile, members of the society dutifully gathered memorabilia about Leadville and Lake County that eventually ended up in the old Carnegie Library, now home to the LCCCA's Heritage Museum on the north end of downtown. The transformation of Leadville's historical consciousness and appreciation had begun.

While the community's historical consciousness started to evolve slowly, Leadville continued to be, well, Leadville. In the mid-1970s, it temporarily revived memories of its fabulous, though not financially successful, Crystal Carnival. The

The spark that led to the creation of this unassuming magazine about Leadville's history also helped provide the impetus to save some of Leadville's irreplaceable historical structures.

Crystal Carnival Association staged a modern-day "Leadville Crystal Carnival." It organized numerous events (*Leadville Crystal Carnival* programs, 1976, 1977), including an "Ice and Snow Driving Contest" featuring a "4 wheel drive division (studded tires permitted), 2 wheel drive open, and Powderpuff Derby (women only)." There was also "Skijoring and Supervised Tubing" with "No age limit" and "No entry fee" as well as broom hockey and cross-country skiing. Talent shows, snow sculptures, live music, casino night, Slavic folk entertainment, youth sledding, ice skating, and snowmobiling were available, too. Sound familiar, these Leadville celebrations? Not surprisingly, many of the winter carnival activities continue to this day, in one form or another, and there is always talk of reviving, in some way, shape, or form, Leadville's renowned 19th-century Crystal Carnival and its ice palace.

In 1978 the population of "urban" Leadville numbered around 4,500. In 1979, the Climax Molybdenum Mine, twelve miles northeast on Fremont Pass, churned along with almost 3,000 full-time employees. Trouble was, Leadville started to look like a one-mine town, with little economic diversity to back it up. "No problem" seemed to be the response as the years passed and Climax kept looking good. When would the Cloud City learn?

On October 6, 1981, Climax's company publication, *Hi Grade*, noted, the Phase III production area of the open pit [Ceresco Ridge] moved a ecord amount of material during the month of September, hauling ?,773,450 tons of material." Now imagine more than 150 miles of work-ngs served by electric locomotives pulling huge ore cars along 30 miles of rack. Then imagine each train hauling 200 tons of ore for a total of 4,000,000 tons in one year. That's a hundred times more than produced by all the Leadville mines in the boom times of 1888. No wonder predic-ions abounded that Climax's huge open-pit ore reserves would last well nto the 21st century. Mining looked good, real good.

Suddenly, Climax Mine unexpectedly started to lay off workers, a lot of workers. People began to worry. Everyone knew about Leadville's long his-ory of gut-wrenching boom-bust cycles, but each bust always seemed to come unexpectedly and be worse than the last. For the next two decades employee reductions and even temporary shutdowns continued in between brief spurts of increased mining activity. Almost unbelievably, Climax — the mining star of Leadville — was in trouble, deep trouble. Once again the world-wide surplus of molybdenum became too large, the demand too small.

By the mid-1980s the work force had dropped down into the hundreds. Soon only skeleton crews were kept on to maintain the mine and guard the equipment. Hundreds of families left Leadville. The local economy reeled. Businesses closed and rumors of Colorado Mountain College's Timberline campus experiencing the same fate circulated. The prices of homes and land in and around Leadville dropped. By 1985, Leadville's population had fallen below 4,000 for the first time since 1878. By the year 2000 (and it was anti-climatic by then), the massive Climax molybdenum mining com-plex had been shut down completely. The smaller, but still important and symbolic Black Cloud Mine, the last mine to remain open in the Leadville Mining District, closed in 1999.

Climax had spent millions of dollars on restoration projects. Yet anyone driving over Fremont Pass can still see the massive swath of mining damage inflicted on this breathtaking mountain vista. Indeed, the Fremont Pass region will remain terribly scarred forever. Some believe that it was worth it, others believe that it was not.

During mining's demise, tourism in Leadville started to pick up. The Leadville Lake County Chamber of Commerce served more than 35,000 visitors in 1984 as compared to 20,000 in 1983. The old multi-media slide production, "The Earth Runs Silver," shown during the summer at the Old Church (originally the Presbyterian Church on Harrison Avenue) was seen by 7,000 people, mostly tourists. What was going on here? More people moving to Colorado — Denver in particular could explain part of the

tourist increase. It seemed logical that another part of the increase could b
attributed to Leadville's incredible historical legacy and its small-town
pristine mountain environment. People outside Leadville and Colorado
were starting, slowly, to look for summer homes, or perhaps an investment
in another potential Aspen or Telluride.

During the 1980s and 1990s other changes in Cloud City occurred
almost imperceptibly. History was now coming to the forefront of
Leadvillites and all Coloradans' consciousness. Don and Jean Griswold, and
other history lovers like Mary B. Cassidy, wrote retrospective columns and
articles for Leadville's *Herald Democrat*. Popular magazines and Colorado
newspapers, especially in Denver, featured Baby Doe, The Matchless Mine
the Tabor Opera House, and more. Then more brochures, pamphlets, and
books about Leadville's incomparable past started to appear on book
shelves throughout Colorado, alongside the mainstays of the 1950s and
1960s — Caroline Bancroft's immensely popular booklets about the Cloud
City and the Tabors ("Hold on to the Matchless!"). In 1980, Edward Blair'
wonderfully conceived, researched, and written, *Leadville: Colorado'
Magic City*, hit the bookstores. It has remained a bestseller ever since. S
too came enjoyable academic books, one of the best being Duane Smith's
Horace Tabor, His Life and Legend. Then came a Leadville history tome
now available on CD-ROM, by Don and Jean Griswold, the story of the ic

*Once called the Hotel Kitchen and the Vendome Hotel, the recently restored
Tabor Grand now carries it original name.*

Built by three brothers from Delaware, the three-story brick Delaware Hotel was erected on Harrison Avenue and Seventh Street. It opened in 1886. In 1890 the lower floor became the R. H. Beggs and Company Dry Goods store. Twelve years later the new owners changed the name to Crews-Beggs Trading Company. Since 1992

this venerable hotel — with its original name — has beckoned visitors to experience Leadville's past glory in its beautifully renovated confines.

Three of the prominent buildings in this old image remain landmarks in Leadville. In the foreground is the "Old Church" (formerly the Presbyterian Church dedicated on December 23, 1889) on upper Harrison Avenue. Beyond is the old High School, now part of the impressive National Mining Hall of Fame and Museum complex on West Ninth Street. In between and partially obscured by the telephone pole crossarms is the elegant Victorian home formerly owned by Augustus Engelbach, proprietor of a successful machine manufacturing company.

palace by Darlene Godat Wier, an examination of the Cloud City's architecture by Lawrence Von Bamford and Kenneth R. Tremblay, Jr., my coffee-table pictorial history, and many others listed in the *Reference* section of this book. Suddenly, readers had a written cornucopia of Leadville history to feast on.

Slowly but surely, hand in hand with the literature, came historical restoration projects up and down Harrison Avenue and elsewhere in town. Many of the projects were partially funded from a portion of the state's gaming tax that was set aside in the newly created State Historical Fund. The Colorado State Historical Society also provided funds for worthy restoration endeavors.

If one had been in a Rip Van Winkle-like sleep since 1980, then awoke to stroll down Harrison Avenue in the early 2000s, the built environment would have looked stunningly different, and all for the better. Indeed, the Tabor Opera House now has good company along Harrison Avenue, dubbed the mainstreet of American mining in the 1880s. The refurbished Tabor Grand has businesses on its lower floor and subsidized apartment housing above. Across the street the beautifully renovated Delaware Hotel beckons overnight patrons. Then comes the proud "Old Church" (formerly the Presbyterian Church dedicated on December 23, 1889), International Odd Fellows Hall, *Herald Democrat* building, Iron Building, Masonic Lodge, National Bank Building, and the Silver Dollar Saloon. The commanding Western Hardware building, which began as the Manville and McCarthy Hardware in August 1881, contains Antiques-Road-Show-like material surrounded

The American National Bank building still stands proudly on the corner of Harrison Avenue and Fifth Street. It is the only remaining bank from Leadville's early financial empire. (Denver Public Library, Western History Department)

by original interior features. Simply walking around in this historic building is worth the time, as it is with so many of the other newly restored buildings in Leadville. A short distance down West Second Street (once infamous State Street) stand the Pastime and Pioneer Saloons. The stories they could tell. Some stories are currently being told in "Doc Holliday's" restored "bordello" on 314-316 Harrison Avenue.

As for the Tabors, Augusta and Horace built a home in Leadville in 1878, which they soon moved to make way for their opera house. Their home is now open for all to see at 116 East Fifth Street. One could also

Shown here are the exterior and interior of the Western Hardware building located immediately south of the Lake County Courthouse on Harrison Avenue. Fortunately, in 1942 Leadville firemen kept the courthouse fire from spreading to this historic edifice. (Below: Lake County Public Library, Colorado Mountain History Collection)

Pack mules about to disembark for a high-country mine wait patiently in front of the Henry H. Tomkins & Co. Hardware, currently the Western Hardware Antique Mall. (Courtesy of Bruce and Hillery McCalister)

The venerable Pioneer Club Bar opened in 1883 at 116 West Second Street. Patrons can still purchase refreshments here on the once-infamous State Street.

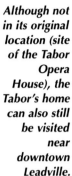

Although not in its original location (site of the Tabor Opera House), the Tabor's home can also still be visited near downtown Leadville.

walk up East Seventh Street to the mythical Matchless Mine, to contemplate the fate of Elizabeth Bonduel Tabor with her visions and hallucinations of thirty years while living in a shack next to the hoist-room and head-frame. A guided tour of the site is available and highly recommended.

Away from downtown, one can drive the short distance to Finntown or Stumpftown and meander through the ghostly remains. Actually, it would be best to take a copy of the *Herald Democrat's* free *Walking Tour* booklet, spend the day, and enjoy the walk. Combine this with some visual imagination and it is easy to step back in time to when Horace Tabor, with Elizabeth at his side, ruled as the uncrowned Silver King of Leadville and the West.

If you want to meet two of Colorado's most intriguing women, you can walk up to the Colorado Historical Society's Healy House Museum and enjoy historical one-woman plays featuring Elizabeth "Baby Doe" Tabor one night, then Augusta Tabor the next. If you want to get a feel for what it was like to be a miner in the early days, the nearby National Mining Hall of Fame and Museum, at 120 West Ninth Street, offers the opportunity in grand style.

Several classic old Leadville homes still stand proudly. At 815 Harrison there is an elegant Victorian home, with its round tower and roof, once owned by Augustus Engelbach, proprietor of a successful machine manufacturing company. Currently it belongs to Mrs. Evelyn Livingston Furman, who also owns the Tabor Opera House. Off Harrison Avenue are numerous beautifully restored homes. Along the first block of West Fourth Street sits "Millionaires' Row" with, among others, well-known Leadville architect

Eugene Robitaille's home, thoroughly and lovingly restored with its under
stated, though elegant lines. One house west stands the unique "Hous
with the Eye," patiently awaiting restoration. On Capitol Hill, the magnif
icent Taylor house towers over the two-mile-high city. The attractive resi
dence at 212 East Ninth Street, neighboring home, and small wood sho₁
were all designed by architect E. H. Dimick. Fanciful 19th-century archi
tectural detailing highlights both Dimick-designed residences. At 21:

West Ninth Street i
architect George King'
eye-catching home. Kin₁
also designed the magnifi
cent 1879 Courthouse
After years of neglect,
home where Benjami₁
Guggenheim lived on th₁
100 block of West Sixtl
Street has been restored
as has been the home o₁
prominent Leadville busi
nessman Benjamin I
Stickley, at 208 Wes
Eighth Street. There is ₁
plethora of other time
honored Leadville home
worth seeing. Many hav₁
been faithfully and wisel₁
preserved. Each has ₁
place in Leadville histor₁
and each has its own his
tory. So too, every year ₁
few more 19th-century
homes are granted nev
lives by yet anothe
modern day prospector

*Architect George King designed several of the
more prominent structures in early Leadville,
including his own home shown here.*

of sorts, in present-day Leadville. Finally, somewhere within each restora
tion project, the spirits of, among others, the members of the first Lak₁
County Civic Center Association reside.

Leadville is also fortunate to have many of its original houses of wor
ship: the Church of the Annunciation, St. George's Episcopal Church, th₁
First Presbyterian Church (now called "The Old Church"), the Firs
Evangelical Lutheran Church, St. Joseph's Church, Temple Israel, and th₁
First Baptist Church. Like the old homes, each church is historically an₁
architecturally interesting in its own right.

Every summer the plaintiff cry of the engine whistle of the old, but newly named, Leadville, Colorado, & Southern Railroad now echoes throughout the valley as the train chugs away from the venerable depot on Hazel Street. From there it rolls along Tenmile Creek, a tributary of the Arkansas River, toward Fremont Pass. The old Colorado & Southern's

steam locomotive No. 641 that faithfully served the line from Leadville to Climax is on display by the depot.

Outdoor opportunities abound near Leadville. Capable four-wheel drive vehicles on approved back-country roads and mountain passes allow access to some of the most rugged and refreshing high-country in America.

The Temple Israel, shown here (above) on the southwest corner of Pine Street and West Fourth Street, is being restored with the help of Colorado Historical Society funds. The Jewish section of the Evergreen Cemetery is also being carefully rehabilitated. Immediately across the street from the Temple Israel is St. George's Episcopal Church (left) erected in 1879.

During the 1920s, Father Jurij Trunk painted a set of unique murals on the walls of St. Joseph's Church on the northeast corner of West Second and Maple Streets. One of them is shown here.

For the hardy, some say insane, there's the Leadville Trail 100 foot race. The starter pulls his gun's trigger at 4:00 a.m. sharp. Non-motorized bike enthusiasts can enjoy a ride along all or some of the 12-mile Mineral Belt Trail that snakes through some of the famous old mining districts. The mountain views are staggering. Interpretative signs enrich the ride. Long-standing Boom Days, which features the Burro Race, remains as a mainstay in early August. In late summer and early fall, fishermen head to nearby Turquoise Lake, Twin Lakes, and numerous small streams. In fall, hunters flock to the dark timber or high-country back-bowls depending on the depth of snow. On Halloween, yet another group of history buffs follow Neil Reynolds on his tour through Leadville's notorious past. In winter, Ski Cooper, and perhaps the memory of the 10th Mountain Division, attracts skiers who enjoy the lower profile and less expensive Colorado ski resort. Piney Creek Nordic Center now offers almost twenty miles of groomed trails for cross-country skiing and snowmobiling. Cross-country ski-trails and huts spread out in mountainous regions in between Leadville, Vail, and Aspen, one of them named for the 10th Mountain Division.

In the 1990s, Leadville made a big decision that has allowed it to retain and preserve so much of its past, and for that matter its present. The Cloud City voted decisively *against* limited-stakes gambling. This decision has enabled historic Leadville to retain, among other things, its small-town atmosphere, something that people are beginning to value more. To wit, take a drive to the gambling towns of Cripple Creek, Central City, or Black Hawk. If you can find a parking spot, take a stroll. These places are gawdy and crowded. No matter what their hype or rationalizations, their historical essences are gone. They have made bargains with the Devil.

Leadville, like most cities, still has crime, drug problems, and simmering ethnic tension, where there should be understanding and cooperation. And Leadville is fast becoming too much of a bedroom community of workers

Once a huge pile of shiny black slag from the Harrison Reduction Works loomed over south Harrison Avenue. Now all that remains is an empty, dreary lot. Many people feel that an integral part of Leadville history was unnecessarily taken away by the Environmental Protection Agency.

for more affluent folks down below in Vail, Beaver Creek, and Avon. There is no way to sugarcoat these issues. Leadville knows that they must be faced and dealt with accordingly. It will not be easy.

During the past decade, the Environmental Protection Agency's (EPA) Superfund has spent millions and millions of dollars in the Leadville Mining District to remove the toxic wastes spewed seemingly everywhere during the heady boom days of the late 19th century. Ironically, the EPA's cleanup efforts themselves have destroyed numerous historical mining areas and created expensive, odd-looking eyesores in their place. Why, too, did the EPA find it necessary to remove the massive slag dump from south Harrison Avenue? It had stood as a silent sentinel over the south end of Harrison Avenue for all time, or so it seemed. Perhaps the EPA has done all this with good reason, and perhaps in the long run it will save lives. Let's hope so. Many of the locals, however, including some influential politicians, believe otherwise.

Still, some people ask incredulously, "So why all this focus on history? What's the big deal? People cannot live on history alone." True, but there is more to it than that. Had Leadville lost its history, it would have lost its unique historical soul. Since 1878 people from all over the world have recognized the name "Leadville." Now more people are beginning to realize

For those who do appreciate Leadville history, there is plenty to see and learn about at the Lake County Civic Center Association's Heritage Museum and Gallery, originally the Carnegie Public Library (shown here), on north Harrison Avenue.

that it is still a special place, thanks to the efforts of a few far-sighted people who looked around several decades ago and realized that some of the great Cloud City's history must be preserved. A good portion of current Leadville natives and newcomers continue to uphold this tradition of historical understanding and respect.

Of course many people will never appreciate or enjoy history. Be thankful for that, or the hordes would overrun and ruin Leadville's small-town atmosphere in a matter of decades. The main point is that there can be prosperous, sustainable lifestyles in Leadville for those who are willing to commit themselves to work and community. They also have Leadville's mesmerizing history and indescribably beautiful mountain scenery as backdrops for their efforts. More people are beginning to realize that history does, indeed, pay. People with money in their pockets will come to see history, experience history, and even make it part of their lives. Consider that the price of homes and land in the Leadville vicinity has more than doubled since the mid-1980s. It appears that Leadville can have it both ways, when its past and present meet.

References

Andrews, J. (1991). Personal communications and resource materials.

Bamford, L. (1987). "Streets of Silver, Leadville's History Through Its Built Environment," *Colorado Heritage*, Vol. 4, 2-29.

Bamford, L. and Tremblay, K. R., Jr. (1996). *Leadville Architecture: Legacy of Silver 1860-1899*. Estes Park, Colorado: Architecture Research Press.

Bancroft, C. (1955). *Augusta Tabor, Her Side of the Scandal*. Boulder, Colorado: Johnson Publishing.

Bancroft, C. (1955). *Silver Queen, The Fabulous Story of Baby Doe Tabor*. Boulder, Colorado: Johnson Publishing.

Bancroft, C. (1960). *Tabor's Matchless Mine and Lusty Leadville*. Boulder, Colorado: Johnson Publishing.

Blair, E. (1980). *Leadville: Colorado's Magic City*. Boulder, Colorado: Pruett Publishing Company.

Blair, E. (1972). *Palace of Ice*. Colorado Springs, Colorado: Little London Press.

Blair, E. (1981). "Ten Years in Retrospect, A Personalized History of the Lake County Civic Center Association," *Mountain Diggings*, 1981, 11, 10-24.

Blair, E. and Churchill, E. R. (1974). *Everybody Came to Leadville*. Gunnison, Colorado: B and B Printers.

Blair, K. (1973). *Ladies of the Lamplight*. Leadville, Colorado: Timberline Books.

Bost, B. (1991-2004). Personal communications and extensive resource materials.

Bunyak, D. (Spring 2003). "Shenandoah-Dives Mining Company, A Twentieth-Century Boom and Bust," *Colorado Heritage*, 35-46.

Burke, J. (1974). *The Legend of Baby Doe*. Lincoln, Nebraska: University of Nebraska Press.

Buys, C. J. (Summer 1998). "Henry M. Teller, Colorado's 'Silver Senator,'" *Colorado Heritage*, 29-36.

Buys, C. J. (1997). *Historic Leadville in Rare Photographs and Drawings*. Ouray, Colorado: Western Reflections Publishing.

Buys, C. J. (1999). *Illustrations of Historic Colorado*. Ouray, Colorado: Western Reflections Publishing.

Buys, C. J. (Summer 1997). "Of Frozen Hydrants and 'Drunkin Sons of Bitches,' Early Leadville's Volunteer Firemen," *Colorado Heritage*, 2-15.

Buys, C. J. (2002). *The Lost Journals of Charles S. Armstrong, From Arkport, New York, to Aspen, Colorado 1867-1894*. Montrose, Colorado: Western Reflections Publishing.

Cain, W. P. (1906). *Mining Claims of Lake County Colorado.* Leadville Colorado: Leadville Publishing and Printing.

Cassidy, M. B. (undated). "Divorce of H. A. W. Tabor." Unpublished manuscript.

Cassidy, M. B. (Ed.) (1977-1984). *Leadville Boom Days.* Series of booklet published by the *Herald Democrat,* Leadville, Colorado.

Cassidy, M. B. (1983). *Off Limits, Leadville in the Early 1940s.* Leadville Colorado: *Herald Democrat.*

Cassidy, M. B. (1974). *St. Joseph's Church and Parish, 1899-1974.* Leadville Colorado: *Herald Democrat.*

Coquoz, R. (1967). *A Century of Medicine in Leadville, Colorado, 1860 1960.* Private Printing.

Coquoz. R. (1969). *King Pleasure Reigned in 1896.* Boulder, Colorado Johnson Publishing.

Coquoz, R. (1967). *Tales of Early Leadville.* Private Printing.

Crofutt, G. A. (1881). *Crofutt's Grip-Sack Guide of Colorado.* Omaha Nebraska: Overland Publishing Company.

Crofutt, G. A. (1885: 1981 reprint). *Crofutt's Grip-Sack Guide of Colorado* Boulder, Colorado: Johnson Publishing.

Davis, C. C. (1916). *Golden Times in Colorado.* Los Angeles, California Phillips Publishing Co.

Dill, R. G. (1881). "History of Lake County" in *History of the Arkansa Valley, Colorado.* Chicago, Illinois: Baskin and Co.

Emmons, S. F., Irving, J. D., and Loughlin, G. F. (1927). *Geology and Ore Deposits of the Leadville Mining District, Colorado.* Washington, D. C. United States Printing Office.

Furman, E. E. L. (1984: 2nd ed.) *The Tabor Opera House, A Captivating History.* Aurora, Colorado: National Writers Press.

Frank Leslie's Illustrated Newspaper (selected issues from 1879 through 1894). New York, New York.

Flynn, N. L. (1959). *History of The Famous Mosquito Pass.* Private Printing

Fogelberg, B. (June 2003). "Harvesting Historical Riches, Leadville's Iron Building," *Colorado History Now.* (Newsletter of the Colorado Historical Society)

Gilfillian, G. and Gilfillian, R. (1964). *Among the Tailings, A Guide to Leadville Mines.* Leadville, Colorado: *Herald Democrat.*

Griswold, D. and Griswold, J. (1996). *History of Leadville and Lake County From Mountain Solitude to Metropolis.* Niwot, Colorado: Colorado Historical Society (in cooperation with the University of Colorado Press).

Griswold, D. and Griswold, J. (1951). *The Carbonate Camp Called Leadville.* Denver, Colorado: University of Denver Press.

Griswold, D. and Griswold, J. (1971). *Herald Democrat.* June 6, 1971.

Hafen, L. and Hafen, A. (1948). *Colorado: A Story of the State and Its People.* Denver, Colorado: Old West Publishing Company.

Harper's New Monthly Magazine (selected issues from 1880). New York, New York.

Harper's Weekly (selected issues from 1859-1892). New York, New York.

Herr, E. and Mayes, J. (1996). "Women and Economic Opportunity in Western Mining Towns in the Late 19th Century: The Case of Leadville, Colorado," *Essays in Economic Business and History,* Vol. 24, 407-423.

Irey, E. F. (1951). *A Social History of Leadville, Colorado, During the Boom Days 1877-1881.* Doctoral dissertation. University of Minnesota.

Karsner, D. (1932). *Silver Dollar, The Story of the Tabors.* New York: Covici Friede.

Kiefer, B. D. (Winter 1997). "Camp Hale: A Civilian Perspective," *Journal of the Western Slope,* Vol. 12 (1), 1-20.

Larsh, E. and Nichols, R. (1993). *Leadville, USA.* Boulder, Colorado: Johnson Books.

Leadville Boomday Booklets. (See Cassidy, M. B.)

Leadville City Directories (1879-1935). Leadville, Colorado: Lake County Public Library.

Leadville Newspapers: *Leadville Daily Herald* (January 1, 1881; October 21, 1881-October 20, 1882), *Herald Democrat* (January 1, 1884; January 1, 1892-June 30, 1892; January 1, 1921-December 31, 1921; January 1, 1942-June 30, 1942), *The Evening News-Dispatch* (March 29, 1903-June 30, 1903).

Manly, N. (1980). "The Influenza Epidmic of 1918-1919," *Mountain Diggings,* 10, 9-14.

Minutes of Meetings of Board of Trustees, Leadville, Colorado. Office of City Clerk, Leadville, Colorado. Volume I (February 28, 1878, through April 11, 1879) and Volume III (August 3, 1880, through July 25, 1882).

Morrell, J. H. (Winter 1997). "Military Memories of Glenn Hanks and the Tenth Mountain Division," *Journal of the Western Slope,* 12(1), 21-34.

Mountain Diggings. (1973-1999). Series of publications by the Lake County Civic Association. Leadville, Colorado (Private printing).

O'Brien, T. (1963). *The Bitter Days of Baby Doe Tabor and Memories of the High Country.* Leadville, Colorado (Private printing).

Philpott, W. (Monograph 10, 1994). "The Lessons of Leadville, Or Why the Western Federation of Miners Turned Left," *Monographs in Colorado History* (Colorado Historical Society).

Riley, M. G. (Spring 2002). "Sin, Gin, and Jasmine, The Controversial Career of Caroline Bancroft," *Colorado Heritage,* 31-46.

Roth, C. (November-December, 1963). "Diary of a Market Hunter," *Colorado Outdoors,* 12 (6).

Rothman, H. K. (1998). *Devil's Bargains, Tourism in the Twentieth-Century American West.* Lawrence, Kansas: University of Kansas Press.

Scribner's Monthly (selected issues from 1876). New York, New York.

Smith, D. A. (1977). *Colorado Mining, A Photographic History.* Albuquerque, New Mexico: University of New Mexico Press.

Smith, D. A. (1989). *Horace Tabor: His Life and Legend.* Boulder, Colorado: University of Colorado Press.

Smith, D. A. (1995-2002). Personal communications.

Smith, D. A. (1992). *Rocky Mountain Mining Camps: The Urban Frontier.* Niwot, Colorado: University Press of Colorado.

Trimble, J. N. (Winter 2001). "The Demons of Elizabeth Tabor: Mining 'Dreams and Visions' from the Matchless," *Colorado Heritage,* 3-21.

Voynick, S. M. (1996). *Climax: The History of Colorado's Climax Molybdenum Mine.* Missoula, Montana: Mountain Press.

Voynick, S. M. (1986). *Leadville, a Miner's Epic.* Missoula, Montana: Mountain Press.

Weir, D. G. (1994). *Leadville's Ice Palace.* Arkansas City, Kansas: Gilliland Printing.

Index

CPSIA information can be obtained
at www.ICGtesting.com
Printed in the USA
FFOW03n1710110917
39849FF